MEXICAN

COOKING CLASS

**BY PATRICIA LAKE
& SHARON LEE BARKHURST**

PHOTOGRAPHER: *Ashley Mackevicius*
FOOD STYLIST: *Anneka Mitchell*

BayBooks
An imprint of HarperCollins*Publishers*

CONTENTS

~

The publishers would like to express their grateful thanks to Elizabeth and Manuel Nila for their assistance during the photographing of this book.

A BAY BOOKS PUBLICATION
An imprint of HarperCollinsPublishers

First published in Australia in 1992 by Bay Books, of
CollinsAngus&Robertson Publishers Pty Ltd (ACN 00 9 913 517)
A division of HarperCollinsPublishers (Australia) Pty Limited
25-31 Ryde Road, Pymble NSW 2073, Australia

HarperCollinsPublishers Limited
77-85 Fulham Palace Road, London W6 8JB, United Kingdom

Copyright © Patricia Lake and Sharon Lee Barkhurst 1992

National Library of Australia
Cataloguing-in-Publication data:

Lake, Patricia
  Mexican Cooking Class.
  Includes index.

  ISBN 1 86378 112 9.

  1. Cookery, Mexican. I. Barkhurst, Sharon Lee. II. Title.
  (Series: Bay Books cooking series).
  641.5972

Food Editor: Anneka Mitchell
Home Economists: Wendy Berecry & Donna Hay
Photographer (cover): Ashley Mackevicius
Food Stylist (cover): Wendy Berecry
Location Photographer: Mark Brewer

Credits:
Tiles thoughout: Country Floors, Woollahra
Plates throughout: Mexican Imports
                  Crazy Horse
                  Albi Imports

Printed in Singapore

5 4 3 2 1
95 94 93 92

MEXICAN CUISINE

Mexican cuisine evokes the tastes and colours of Mexico – a fascinating country that has a rich and diverse culinary history.

When the Spanish conquered Mexico more than 400 years ago they not only found gold, but also corn, beans, chillies, tomatoes, avocados, potatoes, squash, zucchinis and a wealth of new fruits and spices – including pineapples, papayas, peanuts, cocoa and vanilla. They found the cuisines of the Aztec and Mayan Indians sophisticated and exciting – it sent the chefs of Europe running to their kitchens.

In this book we will give you a true taste of Mexico. There are plenty of dishes you will recognise, including the full range of tortillas, tacos, enchiladas and tamales, salsas, barbecued meats and beans; corn and rice recipes. Surprises come in the form of sumptuous seafood dishes, tender roasts and gourmet sauces, including the famous moles; and casseroles of braised meats, poultry and vegetables, which are wonderfully tasty, but also economical.

There are salads like tempting combinations of avocado and papaya, or mixes of pineapple, apple, beets, pinenuts and banana with salad greens. There are crisp vegetables and biting dressings of freshly squeezed lime juice, olive oil and chillies.

Last but not least, there is a stunning array of appetisers and snacks for the 'Coctel' – the Mexican cocktail party. The appetisers are served with a tantalising assortment of fruit drinks and cocktails, many based on the heady Mexican tequila.

THE MEXICAN KITCHEN

Your own kitchen will have everything you need to improvise, but there are some special utensils you can buy if you wish.

Tortilla Press

A small cast iron hand press will simplify tortilla making at home.

You can order a tortilla press through any Mexican restaurant supplier in major cities – the small investment is well worthwhile if you like to make substantial amounts of tortilla for yourself. Otherwise, make tortillas with a rolling pin and roll them out between waxed paper.

Molcajete and Tejolote

The Mexican mortar and pestle. You can get by with a blender or food processor, or even a standard mortar and pestle, but the Mexican type – a round bowl of volcanic rock with three legs and a pestle made from heavy black basalt – is especially good for grinding spices and chillies for sauces. It can be bought in specialist kitchen shops or ordered from Mexican restaurant suppliers.

Cazuelas and Ollas

Mexicans traditionally cook in earthenware casseroles and claypots, called cazuelas and ollas. Good quality heavy-based enamelled pots like the colourful French Le Creuset range are also excellent for Mexican cooking, as are the frypans, and can be used on top of the stove and as ovenware. Baking dishes of flameproof glass are also useful. They all move easily from oven to table and if you use a heat diverter or mat for electric and gas burners you can use Mexican earthenware on stove tops as well as in ovens. Look for them at specialty kitchenware shops.

To season earthenware cazuelas and ollas, rub them with garlic, then fill them with warm water with some oregano, thyme, or bay leaves and bake them in a moderate oven for several hours.

THE MEXICAN PANTRY

As the popularity of authentic Mexican cooking grows, so does the availability of Mexican products. However, you can make do with much of what you already have on your kitchen shelves or in the freezer and what is on sale at good fruit markets and supermarkets.

Herbs and Spices

The essential dried herbs and spices are oregano, coriander, cumin, cloves and chilli powder. Occasionally you will need paprika, dried capsicum (pepper) seeds, aniseed and turmeric.

The only essential fresh herbs are coriander and parsley, both of which are easily available. To make them last longer they should be stored in a jar of water covered with a plastic bag in your refrigerator. Both coriander and parsley are easy to grow at home in pots.

Mexican Foodstuffs – Canned, Dried and Bottled

Prepared fajita (meat strips), marinades, dried Mexican chillies, bottled salsas and other manufactured Mexican products are available at Mexican food suppliers and in the exotic food sections of major department stores. Cans of the many varieties of Mexican chillies, tomatillos (Mexican green tomatoes) nopales (prickly pear leaves), pimiento, hominy (a type of corn for soup) and pastes or powders like mole pablano and pipianes, are exported from Mexico and are usually of excellent quality. Even good cooks in Mexico use them!

Masa Dough and Instant Masa

Instant masa is a pale, fine cornmeal, used to make masa dough for tortillas and tamales. It is available at Mexican suppliers or you can order it in 2 kg bags through some delicatessens and health food stores. It is only an essential ingredient if you want to make your own corn tortillas or tamales. Instant masa is widely available in the United States under the brand name of Masa Harina and is made by the Quaker Oats company. Prepared masa dough is available at some specialist food stores and at Mexican tortilla factories in larger cities.

Corn Meal

A roughly ground corn meal (not masa meal or instant masa), which is an ingredient in corn bread. It is available in health food stores and delicatessens. Italian polenta can also be used.

Fresh Tortillas

Ready-made corn and wheatflour tortillas can be bought by the dozen and frozen in batches to be used for future meals. They are available in larger cities from Mexican food suppliers or tortilla factories, which supply local Mexican restaurants. Phone your local restaurant and ask them where you can buy fresh tortillas. Otherwise, they are sometimes available canned or frozen at some larger supermarkets.

Stocks and Broths

It is handy to have chicken, fish and beef stocks and broths in the freezer. Homemade stock is a good basis for soups and is an essential item to be kept in the freezer for making soup when time is limited. Stock cubes are a suitable substitute, although they may have a saltier flavour.

Oils and Shortening

Mexicans tend to use lard and bacon drippings for cooking. In today's fat and cholesterol-conscious times you may prefer to use olive oil, or the vegetable oil of your choice. We have used the lighter vegetable oils, butter and margarine as shortening throughout this book.

Other Ingredients

Tomatoes, chillies, capsicums (peppers), onions, garlic, cucumbers, lettuce and other salad greens, avocados, sweet corn and zucchini (courgettes) are all excellent stand-bys as are fresh limes, lemons and oranges, grated cheese, fresh eggs, canned tomatoes, tomato paste and puree. Cans of beans and corn are also useful as are green olives, pepitas (pumpkin seeds), peanuts and pine nuts, dried beans, dried chillies, white long grained rice and dark cooking chocolate.

ALL ABOUT CHILLIES

Mexican food is synonymous with chillies and there are dozens of varieties from fiery hot ones to those that are sweet and mild.
If you live near a Mexican food supplier you can experiment with real Mexican chillies, usually available dried in packets, canned, or bottled. But you can make do with any fresh and dried chillies, or even substitute a mixture of capsicums (bell peppers) and dried chilli powder. If you want, make your own dried chillies by threading together different types of fresh chillies and hanging them near a sunny spot by the kitchen window until they are well dried and then store them in an airtight container. As a rule, the smaller the chilli the bigger the bite, and in Mexico this is true of the habenero chilli, which is small, usually green, and deathly hot. There are various ways of spelling chilli – Mexicans use the Spanish word, 'chile', the Americans, 'chili' and other English-speaking countries, 'chilli'. Whatever the spelling, a chilli (or chili pepper), is a member of the genus Capsicum, along with capsicums (bell peppers) and pimientos.

A CHILLI GUIDE
FRESH CHILLIES
Poblano

A reasonably mild dark green chilli, about 10 cm to 12 cm long and used by Mexicans for Stuffed Chillies. When dried the poblano is called an ancho, and sometimes (incorrectly) pasilla pods. When you cannot get poblanos, substitute banana chillies with the insides rubbed with chilli powder.

Jalapeno

This is the most commonly canned and pickled Mexican chilli. It is about 5 cm to 6 cm long, and is fat and juicy. When fresh they can be green, yellow, or reddish. When dried and smoked they are called chipotles, widely available in cans. As a substitute for fresh jalapeno, use any fresh hot chilli.

Serrano

A small, thin, hot, red or green chilli, widely available throughout the world. Mexicans prefer them finely chopped in guacamole and ceviches. Red birdseye chillies can be substituted.

Chile Negro

Also called chilaca, chile negro is long, dark and hot, and when dried is sometimes called chile pasilla. This is difficult to find fresh outside of Mexico and America's border states. If you cannot find them, substitute any dark coloured, medium, hot fresh chilli, or capsicum (pepper) and chilli powder.

Guero

Any pale yellow or green chilli is usually called guero or 'blond'. Small yellow 'wax chillies', usually available bottled, are also known as guero. They are usually fairly hot, and are used fresh or pickled but not dried.

California or Anaheim

Usually mild to medium hot, fresh, long green chillies, which are also called Mexican chillies in some supermarket products. These chillies are suitable for stuffing if you can find any large enough.

Banana Chilli

This is a pale green sweet fresh chilli, about 14 cm to 16 cm long, which ripens to a pale pinky orange. Though it really has a flavour more like a capsicum (pepper) it is useful for stuffing, and is more widely available outside of Mexico than the Mexican pablano chilli. Rub the insides with chilli powder to give the banana chilli a bite.

DRIED MEXICAN CHILLIES

Dried chillies are even richer in Vitamin C than fresh ones and can add special richness and depth to a sauce. Understanding dried chillies is an art form in Mexico – only aficionados can really claim to tell the subtle differences between the dozens of different varieties that are ripened on the vine, sold in packets and exported throughout the world.

Mexican cooks make do with what chillies they can find at their local market and so can you, but try some of the varieties of dried Mexican chillies if you are lucky enough to find a Mexican retailer nearby. You will be amazed at how large and dark some chillies are and how similar a chile ancho, for example, can look to a chile mulato, the drier and darker they become.

As a rule, you usually need to lightly roast or dry-fry the chillies to bring out their flavour, and then soak them in warm water until they soften. But do not soak them too long or you will leave their flavour behind in the water. Do not try to remove their skin, and either slice or puree them with or without their seeds and veins, depending on how much heat you require. Remember the heat in chillies is in their veins, or membranes, not their seeds.

If you cannot find the chilli specified in a recipe, use your own mixture of locally dried chillies, capsicum (pepper), chilli powder or paprika, or substitute one type of dried Mexican chilli for another. Remember few 'gringos', non-South Americans, can really tell the difference between chillies and even cooks in Mexico cannot get every type of chilli they would like. Below is a list of the most common dried Mexican chillies with a brief description of their appearance and flavour.

Chile Ancho

The most commonly used dried chilli in Mexico, the ancho chilli is the pablano ripened to a deep red, and dried. It should still be flexible when dried with a deep reddish brown wrinkled skin. The ancho is easily confused with a mulato which should be more reddish black and not as sharp and fruity as the ancho. Both are large and squat, about 10 cm long by about 8 cm wide. Chile ancho has a sharp flavour but is not a particularly hot chilli. Sometimes ancho chillies are incorrectly labelled as pasilla pods, but the squat shape suggests it is an ancho, not a pasilla.

Chile Guajillo

After chile ancho, the guajillo is the most commonly used dried chilli in Mexico. It is smooth with a tough skin of a deep maroon, long and thin and about 12 cm long. It is medium hot to hot, with a sharp flavour. You may have to discard the skin to puree.

Pasilla or Dried Chile Negro

This is the dried version of the fresh chile negro (black chilli) or chilaca, and is black, shiny and wrinkled. It is long and thin, about 15 cm long and 3 cm wide. Pasilla ranges in flavour from mild to hot and has a rich flavour. Sometimes you will find ancho chillies labelled as pasilla pods, but true chile pasilla or negro, are long and thin, not squat shaped chillies like the ancho.

Chile Mulato

Similar in size and appearance to an ancho chilli, but with a sweeter, more chocolaty taste than the fruitier, sharper flavoured ancho. The mulato is mild to moderately hot and dark reddish-black.

Chile Chipotle

This is the jalapeno chilli, ripened, dried and smoked. Widely available outside of Mexico in jars or cans, they are very hot and are always used with seeds and veins intact.

NOTE REMEMBER TO BE CAREFUL WHEN PREPARING CHILLIES. USE GLOVES, OR CLEAN OUT VEINS AND SEEDS UNDER RUNNING WATERP. DON'T TOUCH YOUR EYES AND BE CAREFUL AROUND SMALL CHILDREN WHEN PREPARING CHILLIES.

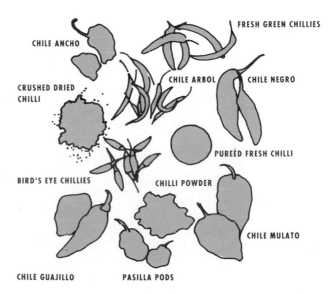

SALSAS
~

SAUCES

No Mexican meal is complete without at least one or two salsas on the table. They are spooned over meats, tacos, eggs and beans; served as dips with totopos (tortilla chips) or corn chips, or poured over enchiladas before baking. Some are made raw to be served immediately like the famous avocado sauce, Salsa de Guacamole, or the fresh tomato, onion and chilli sauce, Salsa Cruda. Others are cooked sauces like Salsa Roja, a fiery condiment to be kept on hand for many meals to come.

The Aztec word for sauce was molli — hence mole — the range of sauces served at Montezuma's table. You will find recipes for moles, which are usually thick, cooked, spicy gravies, throughout this book. In this chapter we have mostly concentrated on the sauces that are derived from the Spanish salsas (sauces). Salsas appear with every meal as a condiment for fish, poultry, meats, tacos and enchiladas or as a dip for corn chips or tortillas.

Red Chilli Sauce

Salsa Roja is widely used as a condiment for fish, poultry, meats, tacos and enchiladas, or as a dip for corn chips or tortillas. Few Mexicans would serve a meal without a Salsa Roja on the table. This sauce will freeze successfully.

Left to right: Fresh Red Chilli Sauce, Pepita Seed Sauce, Avocado Sauce, Cheese Sauce for Tortilla Chips, Green Chilli Sauce

RED CHILLI SAUCE
SALSA ROJA

170 g fresh hot red chillies, seeded

3 cups (750 ml) hot water

3 tablespoons tomato paste

1 garlic clove, crushed

3 tablespoons olive oil

pinch salt

¼ teaspoon ground cumin

1 teaspoon finely chopped fresh oregano

1 teaspoon finely chopped fresh coriander

1 Rinse chillies in cool water. Place in a bowl, cover with hot water and allow to soak for 1 hour. (Alternately steam them for 5 minutes.)

2 Place chillies and remaining ingredients in a food processor or blender with a little extra water and process until coarsely chopped.

3 Place mixture in a saucepan and simmer slowly for 10 minutes, stirring occasionally, or until sauce reaches the desired consistency.

MAKES 3½ CUPS (875 ML)

GREEN CHILLI SAUCE
SALSA VERDE

1 onion, peeled and finely chopped

2 tablespoons vegetable oil

2½ cups (550 g) cooked or canned tomatillos, drained

1 tablespoon finely chopped fresh coriander

2 green California chillies or any large medium to hot green chillies

1 cup (250 ml) chicken stock

1 clove garlic, crushed (optional)

1 Place all ingredients in a food processor or blender and process until smooth.

2 Transfer to a saucepan, season to taste with freshly ground black pepper and salt and simmer for 10 minutes or until sauce reaches desired consistency.

MAKES 3 CUPS (750 ML)

FRESH RED TOMATO AND CHILLI SAUCE
SALSA CRUDA

3 tomatoes, peeled, seeded and chopped.

2 to 3 fresh, large, hot red chillies, seeded and finely chopped

1 onion, peeled and finely chopped

½ teaspoon sugar

2 teaspoons lime or lemon juice

2 tablespoons finely chopped fresh coriander

1 Combine all the ingredients except coriander in a bowl. Cover and stand for at least 1 hour to allow the flavours to develop fully.

2 Stir through coriander and season to taste with freshly ground black pepper and salt.

3 Store in an airtight container in the refrigerator where it will keep for up to 1 week.

MAKES 1½ CUPS (375 ML)

FRESH GREEN CHILLI SAUCE
SALSA VERDE FRESCA

1½ cups (330 g) canned tomatillos, drained and finely chopped

1 onion, peeled and finely chopped

1 clove garlic, crushed

2 fresh or canned large hot green chillies, seeded and finely chopped

1 green capsicum (pepper), finely chopped

½ teaspoon freshly ground black pepper

¼ teaspoon salt

pinch sugar

1 tablespoon lime juice

2 tablespoons finely chopped fresh coriander

1 Combine all ingredients in a bowl, cover and allow to stand for at least 1 hour before serving.

MAKES ABOUT 3 CUPS (750 ML)

VARIATION: For a smooth Fresh Green Chilli Sauce, place ingredients in a food processor or blender and process until smooth. To serve, sprinkle with extra chopped fresh coriander.

≈ TOMATILLOS

Tomatillo, also known as 'husk tomato' or Mexican green tomato, is not an ordinary tomato. Each one is surrounded by a husky, papery leaf and the fruit often appears to be glued into the leaf because of the sap this unusual tropical plant excretes. Tomatillos are zesty in flavour when eaten raw; when cooked they lose their acidic taste but retain their slightly lemony flavour. They are excellent as a sauce, in guacamole, or to flavour moles and meat dishes. Raw tomatillos look great as a garnish and make a wonderful conversation piece on a plate of appetisers. They are widely available canned outside Mexico.

*To microwave: Place
cheeses and sour cream in
a microwave proof bowl
and microwave on
MEDIUM (50%
power) for 1 to 2
minutes. Stir and cook for
1 minute longer or until
cheese melts. Stir through
remaining ingredients
and microwave for 30
seconds longer or until
heated through.*

AVOCADO SAUCE
SALSA DE GUACAMOLE

2 tablespoons pepitas

2 to 3 fresh medium to hot green chillies,
steamed and peeled, or 4 to 6 canned
medium green chillies

small bunch fresh parsley, finely chopped

2 tablespoons finely chopped fresh coriander

3 tablespoons vegetable oil

⅓ cup (80 ml) chicken stock

3 avocados, stoned, peeled and mashed

1 Place pepitas, chillies, parsley and coriander
in a food processor or blender and process until
finely chopped. Add a little chicken stock and
strain, reserving chilli mixture.

2 Heat oil in a frypan and cook chilli mixture
for 1 minute. Add remaining stock, bring to
boil, reduce heat and simmer for 5 minutes.

3 Set aside and allow to cool. Add avocado
and mix until smooth.

Makes 2 to 3 cups (500 to 750 ml)

CHEESE SAUCE
FOR TORTILLA CHIPS
SALSA DE QUESO

1 cup (250 g) ricotta cheese

125 g Cheddar cheese, grated

½ cup (125 ml) sour cream

½ teaspoon ground cumin

pinch dried oregano

1 fresh small chilli, seeded and finely
chopped or ¼ teaspoon chilli powder

1 tomato, peeled, seeded and finely chopped

1 In the top of a double saucepan, melt the
ricotta, cheddar cheese and sour cream over
simmering water, stirring occasionally.

2 Add cumin, oregano, chilli and freshly
ground black pepper to taste. Cook 2 to 3
minutes longer or until heated through and
well combined.

3 Fold in the tomato, heat through and
serve immediately with tortilla chips.

Makes 3 cups (750 ml)

RANCH STYLE CHILLI
SAUCE
SALSA RANCHERA

1 onion, peeled and chopped

2 cloves garlic, crushed

4 large ripe tomatoes, peeled

1 cup (185 g) canned jalapeno chillies

½ teaspoon dried oregano

1 tablespoon finely chopped fresh parsley

1 Place all ingredients in a food processor or
blender and process until fairly smooth.

2 Transfer to a saucepan, bring to the boil,
reduce heat and simmer for 10 to 15
minutes or until sauce reaches desired
consistency.

3 Stand for at least 2 hours before serving to
allow flavours to develop fully.

Makes 2 cups (500 ml)

RED ENCHILADA SAUCE
ENCHILADA SALSA ROJA

3 tablespoons olive oil

2 tablespoons plain flour or instant masa

chilli powder

pinch dried oregano

pinch ground cumin

2 cloves garlic, crushed

2 cups (500 ml) tomato purée

1 cup (250 ml) chicken stock

1 Heat oil in a saucepan. Add flour, chilli
powder, oregano and cumin and cook over a
medium heat, stirring constantly, until
golden brown. Add garlic and tomato purée
and mix to combine.

2 Stir the stock into the tomato and chilli
mixture and bring to the boil, reduce heat
and simmer for 10 minutes, or until sauce
reaches the desired consistency. Store in an
airtight container in the refrigerator for up
to 2 weeks.

Makes 3 cups (750 ml)

Fresh Green Chilli Sauce

GREEN ENCHILADA SAUCE

ENCHILADA SALSA VERDE

2 cups (440 g) canned tomatillos, drained

1 onion, peeled and chopped

2 fresh, small green chillies, seeded and finely chopped

1 clove garlic, crushed

pinch sugar

¾ cup (185 ml) chicken stock

1 Combine tomatillos, onions, chillies, garlic and sugar in a saucepan. Cook over a low heat, stirring constantly, for 6 to 8 minutes.

2 Place tomatillo mixture and chicken stock in a food processor or blender and process until smooth.

3 Return mixture to saucepan and simmer for 5 minutes, stirring constantly, or until sauce reaches desired consistency. Store in an airtight container in the refrigerator for up to 2 weeks.

MAKES 2 CUPS (500 ML)

PEPITA SEED SAUCE

SALSA DE PEPITA

100 g pepitas, toasted

2 fresh small green chillies, seeded

small bunch fresh parsley, finely chopped

2 cups (500 ml) chicken stock

1 Place pepitas, chillies, parsley and stock in a food processor or blender and process until smooth.

2 Transfer to a saucepan, bring to the boil and cook for 1 minute, stirring constantly, or until heated through and well combined.

MAKES 2 CUPS (500 ML)

APERITIVOS

APPETISERS AND SNACKS

Appetisers came into their own when North Americans introduced the cocktail party to Mexico and *¡Olé!* the coctel was born – an excuse to have a party and delight in an endless variety of colourful concoctions, while feasting on a sumptuous array of appetisers and snacks – the ultimate finger foods.

In fact the Mexican coctel is much more an eating event than the cocktail party tends to be in most countries. It begins early evening when the satisfaction of the heavy noon meal has worn off, and continues until ten at night – when it is time for a late supper.

There are also several 'pan' or bread recipes in this section including the Bolillo or French Roll, which is the basis for tortas (Mexican submarine sandwiches). Yeast breads are often served as a snack or like Pan de Muerto (Bread of the Dead), as a special treat for a festive day.

For the most part Mexican snacks are fresh, mouthwatering toppings on a variety of tortillas and pastries and served with spicy salsas, all designed to tantalise the appetite.

Left to right: Seasoned Jalapino Chillies, Savoury Toasted Pepitas, Peanuts with Chilli

AVOCADO DIP
GUACAMOLE

Mexicans combined the Aztec words for avocado and mixture, aguacate and mole, to make guacamole. Serve as a dip with corn chips or as a creamy condiment with any Mexican meal.

2 large ripe avocados stoned and peeled

2 teaspoons finely chopped onions

1 garlic clove, crushed

2 tablespoons lemon or lime juice

½ teaspoon salt

1 tomato, peeled, seeded and finely chopped

2 tablespoons sour cream or mayonnaise

2 teaspoons finely chopped fresh coriander (optional)

1 to 3 hot red chillies (depending on taste), seeded and finely chopped or ½ teaspoon chilli powder (optional)

1 Mash avocados with a fork. Add remaining ingredients and mix well to combine.

2 Serve in a wooden or stone bowl with wedges of tomato and corn chips, garnished with coriander leaves.

MAKES 2 CUPS (500 ML)

SIMPLE AVOCADO DIP
GUACAMOLE SENCILLO

3 large ripe avocados, stoned and peeled

1 medium onion, peeled and finely chopped

2 hot red chillies, seeded and finely chopped

⅓ cup (80 ml) lemon juice

dash Tabasco sauce

1 tablespoon chopped fresh coriander

1 Mash avocados with a fork. Add remaining ingredients, season to taste with freshly ground black pepper and salt and mix well to combine.

2 Garnish with chopped fresh coriander and serve with tortilla chips if desired.

MAKES 2 CUPS (500 ML)

≈ **SPICY CHICKEN ROLLS**

Spicy chicken rolls are sold around bus and train stations and by enterprising vendors in Mexico who push them at you through the windows whenever you stop at a station. Some vendors will even jump on the train and rush through the aisles selling as they go, jumping off at the next station to ply their delicious wares on the return journey.

RANCH STYLE EGG FEAST
HUEVOS RANCHEROS PARA FIESTA

2 tablespoons olive oil

2 onions, peeled and finely chopped

2 cloves garlic, crushed

2 red or green capsicums (peppers), finely chopped

1 to 2 fresh small red chillies, seeded and finely chopped

1 teaspoon ground cumin

1 teaspoon dried oregano

4 large tomatoes, peeled and chopped

½ cup (125 ml) tomato purée

½ teaspoon sugar

½ cup (125 ml) chicken stock

12 eggs

2 tablespoons chopped fresh coriander

1 Heat oil in a heavy-based pan and cook onion, garlic, capsicum, and fresh chilli over a medium heat for 4 to 5 minutes or until onion is soft. Add cumin, oregano and chilli powder and sugar, stir well and cook for 1 minute longer. Add tomatoes, tomato purée and chicken stock. Bring to the boil, reduce heat and simmer for 5 to 10 minutes or until sauce reaches a thick soup consistency.

2 Pour sauce into a greased 8-cup (2 litre) capacity, ovenproof dish. Using a spoon, make a well in the sauce and break an egg carefully into it. Repeat with remaining eggs, placing them deep into the sauce to make room for the remaining ones.

3 Bake at 180°C (350°F) for 10 to 15 minutes or until eggs are cooked to your liking. Sprinkle with coriander and serve with warmed tortillas, avocado slices, rice and refried beans, if desired.

SERVES 6

VARIATION: You may like to serve this dish in six individual ramekins. Divide sauce between ramekins and break 2 eggs into each. Cook for 8 to 10 minutes.

Ranch Style Egg Feast

SPICY CHICKEN ROLLS
TORTAS COMPUESTA

6 Mexican bolillos or small French bread rolls

½ cup (125 g) refried beans

2 to 3 lettuce leaves, shredded

3 cooked chicken breast fillets, shredded

300 g mild cheese, grated

chilli powder

Seasoned Jalapeno Chillies

1 Cut bread rolls in half and hollow out bottom half of roll leaving a 1 cm shell.

2 Spread beans over bottom half of roll and top with lettuce and chicken. Sprinkle with cheese and chilli powder to taste.

3 Place under a preheated medium grill and cook for 2 to 3 minutes or until cheese melts. Serve with Seasoned Jalapeno Chillies.

SERVES 6

Spicy Empanadas

SPECIAL MEXICAN SANDWICHES
TORTAS ESPECIAL

6 Mexican bolillos or small French rolls, split in half and buttered

6 thick rashers bacon, trimmed

1 small avocado, stoned and peeled

1 teaspoon lime juice

6 slices Cheddar cheese

1 small Spanish onion, peeled and finely sliced

2 to 3 lettuce leaves, shredded

½ cup (125 ml) sour cream

2 teaspoons Red Chilli Sauce or Green Chilli Sauce or dash Tabasco sauce

6 jalapeno chillies, seeded and cut into thin strips

≈ **SWEET EMPANADAS**

Substitute meat fillings with jams, preserves, mincemeat, or a sweet filling of your choice. Prepare empanadas as above and sprinkle tops with sugar before baking.

1 Toast rolls under a preheated grill for 1 to 2 minutes or until golden.

2 Cook bacon in a pan over a medium high heat for 3 to 4 minutes or until crisp. Drain on absorbent paper.

3 Mash avocado with lime juice. Spread over bottom half of rolls. Top with bacon, cheese, onion, lettuce, a spoonful of sour cream and chilli sauce to taste.

4 Serve immediately, each garnished with jalapeno chillies.

SERVES 6

SPICY EMPANADAS
EMPANADAS DE PICADILLO

Empanadas are little pastry turnovers stuffed with savoury or sweet fillings. In Mexico, empanadas are sold by street vendors, in markets and at panadarias. The savoury ones are often served with a red or a green chilli sauce

750 g readymade shortcrust pastry
vegetable oil for cooking

FILLING

2 teaspoons oil
1 clove garlic, crushed
250 g minced beef
250 g minced pork
½ cup (125 ml) tomato purée
⅓ cup (80 ml) sherry
1 teaspoon ground allspice
1 teaspoon ground cumin
1 teaspoon ground cinnamon
½ teaspoon ground cloves
1 tablespoons sugar
1 tablespoon freshly squeezed lime or lemon juice
125 g slivered almonds

1 TO MAKE FILLING: heat oil in a pan and cook garlic for 1 minute. Add beef and pork and cook over a medium high heat for 4 to 5 minutes or until browned. Add tomato purée, sherry, allspice, cumin, cinnamon, cloves, sugar and lime juice. Reduce heat and simmer, uncovered, for 20 minutes, stirring occasionally, until most of the liquid evaporates. Add almonds and set aside to cool.

2 Roll pastry out to 3 mm thickness and cut out ten 12 cm circles, using an upturned saucer as a guide

3 Place a spoonful of mixture on one side of each pastry round. Moisten pastry edges with a little water. Fold over to enclose and press edges firmly together with a fork to seal.

4 Heat enough oil in a deep pan to cover base by 3 cm to 5 cm and cook pastries for 4 to 5 minutes or until golden brown and cooked through. Alternatively, bake at 190°C (375°F) for 15 to 20 minutes.

5 Serve with Red or Green Chilli Sauce.

SERVES 4

CHEESY CORN CHIPS
NACHOS

200 g tortilla corn chips
2 cups (500 g) refried beans
125 g Cheddar cheese, grated
1 small onion, peeled and finely chopped
½ cup (125 ml) sour cream
½ cup (125 ml) chilli sauce
½ cup (125 ml) guacamole (optional)

1 Arrange tortilla chips on a large oven-proof serving plate and dot with refried beans.

2 Sprinkle with cheese and cook at 180°C (350°F) for 10 to 15 minutes or until cheese melts.

3 Spoon over sour cream and chilli sauce. Serve with a side dish of guacamole, if desired.

SERVES 4

EGGS RANCH STYLE
HUEVOS RANCHEROS

2 tablespoons vegetable oil
2 medium corn or wheat flour tortillas
2 eggs
4 tablespoons Ranch Style Chilli Sauce
1 small avocado, stoned, peeled and sliced
3 tablespoons refried beans (optional)

1 Heat oil in a heavy-based pan and cook tortillas until crisp. Drain on absorbent paper. Set aside to keep warm.

2 Poach or fry eggs and place on tortillas. Top with chilli sauce and avocado slices.

3 Serve with a side dish of refried beans, if desired.

SERVES 1

≈ **CRUNCHY TORTILLAS–TOSTADAS**

Make tostadas by cooking flat corn or wheat flour tortillas in hot oil in a heavy-based pan until they become golden brown and crunchy. Drain on absorbent paper. They are used as a base for guacamole, shredded chicken, seafood, pork and beef, and make great party finger foods or a sumptuous snack any time of day! Use small to medium sized tortillas to make snack-sized tostadas One large tortilla will make a meal-sized tostada – an impressive centrepiece for the table.

SAVOURY TOASTED PEPITAS
PEPITAS TOSTADA

30 g butter or margarine

1 to 2 cloves garlic, crushed

¼ teaspoon chilli powder

250 g pepitas

1 tablespoon Worcestershire sauce

1 Melt butter in a large heavy-based pan and cook garlic and chilli powder over a medium heat for 1 minute.

2 Add pepitas and cook, stirring constantly, until they have all popped. Add Worcestershire sauce and mix well to combine. Season to taste with salt if desired.

3 Serve warm or cold.

MAKES 250 G

THE DEVIL'S SANDWICH
TORTA DIABLO

These very hot delights are popular in the markets of Guatalajara, Mexico's second largest city in the state of Jalisco.

50 g butter or margarine

6 large French or Italian bread rolls, split in half

2 cups (500 g) shredded cooked beef, chicken or pork

1 small onion, peeled and finely chopped

3 cups (750 ml) Red Chilli Sauce, warmed

1 Melt butter or margarine in a pan and cook rolls on each side over a medium heat until golden brown. Remove and set aside to keep warm.

2 Add shredded beef to pan and cook until heated through. Place cooked beef on the bottom half of the rolls, sprinkle with onion and top with roll

3 Quickly dip whole roll in warmed Red Chilli Sauce and serve immediately, accompanied by jalapeno chillies and shredded lettuce, if desired.

SERVES 6

MEXICAN BREAD ROLLS
BOLILLOS

The bolillo can be split in half and filled with an infinite variety of ingredients to make the definitive submarine sandwich – Torta Ezpecial

1½ cups (375 ml) boiling water

50 g butter or margarine

30 g sugar

½ teaspoon salt

1 tablespoon dried yeast

¼ teaspoon caster sugar

3 tablespoons warm water

5 cups (625 g) plain flour

½ teaspoon salt dissolved in 1 tablespoon water

1 Place boiling water, butter or margarine, sugar and salt in a large mixing bowl and stir until butter or margarine melts and sugar and salt dissolves. Set aside and allow to cool.

2 Combine yeast, caster sugar and warm water and mix until yeast dissolves. Cover and set aside in a warm, draft-free place for 5 to 10 minutes or until mixture is frothy.

3 Add yeast mixture to cooled butter mixture. Add 2½ cups (375 g) flour and mix to form a stiff batter. Cover and allow to stand in a warm draught-free place until batter rises and becomes spongy.

4 Add remaining flour to form a stiff dough. Turn on to a lightly floured surface and and knead for 5 to 8 minutes or until smooth and elastic.

5 Place dough in a lightly greased bowl, cover with plastic wrap and allow to stand in a warm draught-free place for 1 hour or until dough doubles in size.

6 Punch down and turn on to a lightly floured surface and knead for 1 minute longer. Wrap in plastic wrap and set aside to rest for 5 minutes.

7 Divide the dough into 10 portions. Shape each portion into a small submarine shape.

8 Place rolls on greased oven trays and cover loosely with plastic wrap and set aside in a warm draught-free place for 30 to 45 minutes or until doubled in size.

9 Brush each roll lightly with salted water mixture and bake at 190°C (375°F) for 20 to 25 minutes or until golden and base sounds hollow when tapped with fingertips.

MAKES 10 ROLLS

MEXICAN CORN BREAD
PAN DE MAIZ

60 g butter
1 onion, peeled and finely chopped
1 to 2 fresh small chillies, finely chopped
1 egg
1 cup (250 ml) milk
1 cup (250 g) creamed corn
1 cup (175 g) polenta (cornmeal)
1 cup (125 g) plain flour
1½ teaspoons baking powder
1 teaspoon salt
60 g Cheddar cheese, grated

1 Melt butter in a frypan and cook onion and chilli over a medium heat for 3 to 4 minutes or until onion is soft. Set aside.

2 Whisk together egg and milk. Add corn and mix well.

3 Sift together polenta, flour, baking powder and salt into a mixing bowl. Add chilli mixture, egg mixture and cheese and mix until just combined.

4 Spoon into a greased and lined 20 cm square cake pan and bake at 180°C (350°F) for 30 to 35 minutes or until golden and cooked when tested with a skewer.

SERVES 4

≈ **PAN BREADS**

Mexico's traditional bread is the tortilla, but yeast and wheat flour breads brought by the Spanish and French settlers are also popular, but more as a snack or treat on a fiesta day, than as a staple. Pan de Muerto for example, is only served once a year, on All Saints Day. Panadrillas or village bakeries are found all over Mexico, where an array of breads and sweet cakes are baked every morning, leaving a tantalising aroma throughout the streets. Bread vendors also sell from door-to-door, carrying their large, flat, woven baskets filled with loaves and pastries, and covered with brightly coloured serviettas.

Mexican Corn Bread

This bread is traditionally served on the festive All Saints Day, when Mexicans pay respects to their departed family members.
Mexican culture embraces mortality and Mexicans have a strong belief in the afterlife. Rather than mourn their dead they celebrate death, so on All Saints Day they like to have a party. People line the streets for the fiesta. Skull-shaped candies are sold on every corner, and at night there is street dancing and fireworks.

BREAD OF THE DEAD
PAN DE MUERTO

1 teaspoon dried yeast

3 tablespoons warm water

4 cups plain flour, sifted

1 teaspoon salt

⅓ cup caster sugar

125 g butter or margarine, cut into pieces

1 tablespoon finely grated orange rind

1 tablespoon finely grated lime or lemon rind

6 eggs, lightly beaten

GLAZE

½ cup (125 g) sugar

3 tablespoons water

1 Dissolve yeast in warm water. Cover and set aside in a draught-free place for 5 to 10 minutes or until mixture is frothy.

2 Sift flour, salt and sugar together into a bowl. Rub in butter with fingertips until mixture resembles fine breadcrumbs. Stir through orange and lemon rinds. Make a well in the centre and add yeast mixture and eggs. Mix to a soft dough.

3 Turn onto a floured surface and knead for 5 minutes or until smooth and elastic. Place dough in a large greased bowl, cover with plastic wrap and set aside in a warm draught-free place for 1 to 1¼ hours or until doubled in bulk.

4 Turn onto a floured surface and knead for 2 minutes longer. Divide dough into 4 portions and separate a small ball from each portion. This will become the bones to decorate the bread

5 Shape the four large portions into balls and place on a greased and floured oven tray. Flatten slightly with palm of hand. Shape smaller portions of dough each into 2 bones. Brush surface of larger portions lightly with water and place bones on top to form crossbones.

6 Cover with plastic wrap and set aside in a warm, draught-free place for 45 to 60 minutes or until a fingerprint pressed in to dough remains. Bake at 180°C (350°C) for 30 to 35 minutes or until golden brown and bread sounds hollow when tapped on the base with fingertips.

7 TO MAKE GLAZE: Place sugar and water in a pan and cook over a low heat, stirring constantly, until sugar dissolves. Bring to the boil and cook for 1 minute. Brush hot rolls with glaze and sprinkle with a little extra sugar.

MAKES 4 LOAVES

Tortilla Chips with Guacamole

≈ **BAKED CORN CHIPS**

If you like freshly made corn chips but are mindful of calories and cholesterol, bake them instead of deep frying them.

CORN CHIPS OR FRIED TORTILLA CHIPS
TOTOPOS FRITOS

12 fresh and soft corn tortillas, quartered

vegetable oil for cooking

salt to taste

1 Heat oil in a heavy-based pan and cook tortilla pieces until golden crisp. Drain on absorbent paper.

2 Sprinkle with salt to taste, allow to cool and serve with your favourite salsa or guacamole.

NOTE: The tortillas can be salted before they are cooked. Brush both sides with a mixture of 2 teaspoons of salt and 3 tablespoons of water. Set aside and allow to dry completely before cooking.

SERVES 4

SEASONED JALAPENO CHILLIES
JALAPENOS CON ESPICES

3 tablespoons lemon pepper

3 tablespoons coarse salt

1 cup (185 g) canned jalapeno chillies, drained

1 small onion, peeled and thinly sliced into rings (optional)

1 Combine lemon pepper and salt. Place in the centre of a serving plate and arrange chillies and onion rings

SERVES 4

SOPAS
~

SOUPS

Soup signals the start of the main meal of the day, and in Mexico it is in the early afternoon, before siesta. Mexican soups are designed to prime your appetite for the feast to come.

There are two kinds of soup. Wet soups (sopas aguadas) are like the soups we are used to. Dry soups (sopas secas) are rice or noodle dishes that have absorbed the soup stock or broth in which they were cooked. You will find them in the chapter on Rice, Bean and Corn Dishes.

Mexicans begin with a sopa aguada and then follow with a sopa seca, before the main courses.

There are exceptions. The following recipes include the famous Pozole, the national favourite reflecting yet again the Mexican love of corn, and which is really a meal in itself. Pozole is more a hearty supper dish than a starter to a meal.

Pork and Hominy Soup

≈ POZOLE

Hominy is prepared from large white dried corn kernels which you can buy in Mexican markets, but otherwise it is available canned at most good delicatessens. Cooked in a huge soup pot and left to simmer all day long, Pozole has many variations, which contain pork, turkey or chicken. In Mexico they use the pig's head for a full-flavoured stock. Sometimes ordinary corn is used instead of hominy

PORK AND HOMINY SOUP
POZOLE

Pozole is a popular supper dish and is often served at fiestas to celebrate birthdays or weddings, or at Christmas time.

1 kg pork shoulder, cut into large pieces

3 litres water

2 x 500 g cans hominy or corn kernels, drained

2 onions, peeled and finely chopped

1 teaspoons salt

2 cups shredded cabbage, or ½ small cabbage, shredded

8 spring onions, finely chopped

2 carrots, peeled and grated

2 tomatoes peeled, seeded and finely chopped

3 radishes, chopped

3 limes, cut into wedges

3 fresh hot red or green chillies, finely chopped

chilli sauce, readymade or homemade

1 Place pork, water, hominy, onion and salt in a large, heavy based saucepan. Bring to the boil, reduce heat and simmer for 2 to 3 hours, or until the meat is tender.

2 Remove pork from soup and cool. Shred meat. Skim fat from surface of cooled soup. Return shredded meat to soup and reheat.

3 Serve cabbage, spring onions, carrots, tomatoes, radishes, chillies, limes and chilli sauce in separate bowls for each person to serve themselves.

SERVES 6

VARIATION: Substitute 2 medium chickens or 1 small turkey for pork. When chicken and turkey are cooked, debone, then add meat to soup.

ZUCCHINI (COURGETTE) SOUP

SOPA DE CALABRACITAS

8 small zucchinis (courgettes), trimmed

6 cups (1½ litres) beef stock

50 g butter

1 onion, peeled and finely chopped

1 tablespoon plain flour

½ cup (125 ml) cream

CROUTONS
3 tablespoons vegetable oil

6 slices stale bread with crusts removed, cubed

1 Place zucchini and stock in a large saucepan, bring to the boil, reduce heat and simmer for 5 minutes.

2 Remove zucchini and chop into small pieces. Set stock aside.

3 Melt butter in a frypan and cook onion over a medium heat for 4 to 5 minutes or until soft. Remove from heat.

4 Combine ½ cup (125 ml) reserved stock and flour and whisk until smooth. Gradually add to onion, stirring constantly.

5 Heat remaining stock in a saucepan over a low heat. Add chopped zucchini and flour and onion mixture and cook, stirring constantly until soup thickens. Simmer 10 minutes. Season to taste with freshly ground black pepper and salt.

6 **TO MAKE CROUTONS:** Heat oil in a frypan and cook bread cubes on all sides until golden. Just prior to serving, stir through cream and sprinkle with croutons.

SERVES 4 TO 6

Left to right: Prawn Soup, Chicken and Corn Soup, Chilled Avocado Soup, Mexican Gazpacho

≈ SQUASH FLOWERS

When in season, fresh squash or zucchini (courgette) flowers are often used in Mexican cuisine, especially in soups and salads and as a garnish for casseroles. You need to cook them as soon as possible after picking. Otherwise you can buy them canned at speciality Mexican outlets.

BEAN SOUP
SOPA DE FRIJOLES

This soup, sometimes called 'poor man's soup', can be made with the beans of your choice.

1 cup (220 g) pinto or kidney beans, washed and soaked for 8 hours

6 cups (1½ litres) water

1 onion, peeled and finely sliced

2 canned tomatoes, chopped

1 clove garlic, crushed

½ teaspoon dried oregano

1 teaspoon chilli powder

3 slices stale bread with crusts removed cubed and cooked in garlic oil until golden

1 Drain and place beans in a heavy-based saucepan. Add enough water to cover them. Bring to the boil, reduce heat and simmer for 5 hours, adding more water during cooking when necessary.
2 Add onion, tomatoes, garlic, oregano and chilli powder after 2½ hours of cooking. Continue to simmer.
3 When beans are tender, strain, reserving stock and place in a food processor or blender with a little stock and process until smooth.
4 Return to pan with stock, and reheat. Add some extra boiling water if soup is too thick. To serve, sprinkle with croutons, chopped onions, and coriander.

SERVES 4

≈ **MEXICAN - INDIAN SOUP**

This is a simple chicken stock which is made into a substantial meal by the addition at the table of shredded chicken, cooked rice and chick peas, and lots of fresh herbs.

CHICKEN AND AVOCADO SOUP
SOPA DE POLLO Y AGUACATE

vegetable oil for cooking

4 medium corn tortillas, cut into 1½ cm wide strips

20 g butter

1 small onion, peeled and chopped

100 g small fresh green chillies, steamed and chopped or 150 g canned green chillies, drained and chopped

6 cups (1½ litres) chicken stock

2 cooked chicken breast fillets, shredded

2 ripe avocados

1 tablespoon chopped fresh coriander

1 Heat oil and cook tortilla strips until crisp. Drain on absorbent paper and set aside.
2 Melt butter in a heavy-based stockpot and cook onion and chillies over a medium heat for 4 to 5 minutes or until onions are soft.
3 Add stock and shredded chicken. Bring to the boil, reduce heat and simmer, covered, for 15 minutes.
4 Stone, peel and slice avocados. Serve soup in individual bowls garnished with tortilla strips and avocado slices. Sprinkle with coriander leaves.

SERVES 4

MEXICAN-INDIAN SOUP
CALDO DE INDIANO

1½ kg chicken pieces

16 cups (4 litres) water

3 cloves garlic

2 large onions, peeled and quartered

4 carrots, peeled and quartered

2 tablespoons chopped fresh parsley

2 cups (310 g) rice, cooked

1 cup (250 g) chick peas, cooked

6 spring onions, finely chopped

3 tablespoons finely chopped fresh coriander

3 fresh hot chillies, finely chopped

4 limes cut into wedges

1 Place chicken, water, garlic, onion, carrot, parsley and freshly ground black pepper and salt to taste in a large heavy-based saucepan. Bring to the boil, reduce heat and simmer for 30 to 45 minutes until chicken is cooked through. Remove chicken from stock and shred. Set aside. Strain the stock and keep hot.

2 **To Serve:** Place a little rice, chick peas, and shredded chicken in each bowl and ladle over chicken stock. Place spring onions, coriander, chillies, and wedges of limes in separate bowls for each person to garnish their soup as they wish.

Note: Any remaining stock can be frozen for later use.

Serves 6 to 8

CHILLED AVOCADO SOUP
SOPA DE AGUACATE

3 large ripe avocados

1¼ cups (310 ml) cream

½ cup (125 ml) milk

1 cup (250 ml) chicken stock

1½ tablespoons fresh lemon juice

Tabasco sauce, to taste

chopped fresh chives, to garnish

1 Stone and peel avocados. Place in a food processor or blender with fresh cream, milk and chicken stock and process until smooth. Add lemon juice, Tabasco and freshly ground black pepper and salt. Process to combine.

2 Refrigerate until well chilled. Serve in a large soup tureen. Garnish with chives or coriander leaves and accompany with a bowl of sour cream.

Serves 4 to 6

SOUP FOR CHRISTMAS EVE
SOPA DE NOCHE BUENA

8 cups (2 litres) chicken stock

300 g chicken breast fillets

1 small tomato, peeled, seeded and chopped

1 spring onion, chopped

1 red capsicum (pepper), chopped

1 small corn tortilla

2 tablespoons (40 ml) sherry

½ cup (125 ml) fresh cream, whipped

1 Heat stock in a deep frypan and poach chicken for 10 minutes or until tender. Remove chicken and set aside to cool. Cut into small pieces and set aside.

2 Transfer stock to a heavy-based saucepan. Add tomato, the spring onion and capsicum. Bring to the boil, reduce heat and simmer for 30 minutes.

3 Place tortilla in a food processor or blender and process until finely ground. Add to stock and cook until thickened.

4 Return chicken to soup and simmer for a further 3 minutes. Stir through sherry just before serving. Spoon into individual bowls and top with a spoonful of whipped cream.

Serves 6

MEXICAN GAZPACHO
GAZPACHO MEXICANA

This famous chilled Spanish soup takes on new meaning when translated into Mexican cuisine! The Mexicans sometimes reduce the amount of tomato juice and eat their gazpacho as a salad.

1 tablespoon ground almonds

1 garlic clove, crushed

1 tablespoon olive oil

1 kg ripe tomatoes, peeled, seeded and finely chopped

1 small onion, peeled and finely chopped

1 small cucumber, finely diced

1 cup (250 ml) tomato juice

2 tablespoons red wine vinegar

2 tablespoons fresh lime juice

3 tablespoons finely chopped fresh parsley

2 tablespoons finely chopped fresh coriander

GARNISH
fresh lime wedges

chopped serrano chillies

fresh coriander leaves

1 Combine ground almonds, garlic and oil to form a smooth paste.

2 Place tomatoes in a bowl, add almond paste and remaining ingredients. Mix well, taking care not to crush the tomatoes. Chill for at least 2 hours before serving.

3 Serve in individual bowls with a small amount of ice. Accompany with wedges of lime and sprinkle with fresh chopped serrano chillies and coriander leaves.

SERVES 4 TO 6

STEP-BY-STEP TECHNIQUES

SPICED LAMB SOUP
SOPA DE BIRRIA

½ cup (125 ml) olive oil

2½ to 3 kg leg of lamb

3 banana leaves, for wrapping lamb (if unavailable, use foil)

750 g dried masa or instant masa, mixed with 1 teaspoon salt and enough warm water to form a thick paste

3 tomatoes, peeled and quartered

3 to 4 onions, peeled and chopped

2 cloves garlic

½ teaspoon dried oregano

2 tablespoons vegetable oil

8 cups (2 litres) chicken stock

1 onion, peeled and finely diced

fresh coriander, finely chopped

thin slices of lime

PASTE
2 fresh hot chillies

2 cups (500 ml) water

3 ancho chillies roasted, seeded and de-veined or 2 medium green capsicums (peppers)

6 cloves garlic

1 white onion, peeled and quartered

½ teaspoon cumin seeds

¼ teaspoon ground ginger

1½ teaspoons dried oregano

3 whole cloves

1 teaspoon ground allspice

1 small stick cinnamon

1 sprig fresh thyme

1 large bay leaf

1 Rub olive oil over lamb. Set aside.

2 TO MAKE PASTE: Place fresh chillies and water in a saucepan. Bring to the boil, reduce heat and simmer for 20 minutes. Drain and reserve water. Place ancho and fresh chillies, garlic, onion, cumin, ginger, oregano, cloves, allspice, cinnamon, thyme and bay leaf in a food processor or blender and process to form a thick paste. Season to taste with freshly ground black pepper and salt.

3 Spread spice paste over lamb, set aside and allow to stand for 30 minutes.

4 Spread banana leaves with masa mixture. Wrap lamb in leaves and place in a roasting pan.

5 Place roasting pan in a bain marie (water bath) and bake at 180°C (350°F) for 2 to 3 hours or until mutton is tender adding water to bath when necessary.

6 Place tomatoes, onions, garlic and oregano in a food processor or blender and process until combined. Heat oil in large saucepan and add tomato mixture. Cook over a low heat for 25 minutes. Add stock and simmer for 25 minutes longer.

7 Add pan juices from lamb to soup. Shred cooked lamb while still hot and divide between individual serving bowls. Ladle over soup and serve sprinkled with onion, fresh coriander and limes. Serve with tortillas.

SERVES 4 TO 6

Traditionally, mutton is the preferred meat for Sopa de Birria. If it is available to you, by all means use it. Ready accessibility to good quality lamb, however, and a preference for its more subtle flavours, make it an ideal substitute.

Birria is a rustic soup made from wrapped and roasted (barbacoa-style) mutton or lamb and served in a rich broth garnished with fresh herbs and eaten with tortillas.

Spread spice over lamb

Spread banana leaves with masa mixture, and wrap leaves around lamb

Spiced Lamb Soup

ANTOJITOS

~

TACOS, ENCHILADAS AND TAMALES

Probably the type of Mexican food best known outside of Mexico is what the Mexicans themselves call antojitos – 'little whims' or cravings.

The word antojito literally means 'a capricious whim or desire', and these dishes which are mostly based on the tortilla corn dough, masa, are really traditional Mexican fast food, on sale at marketplaces and at fetes and bazaars. Antojitos also appear at the late evening meal of the day when supper calls for just a little something to finish the day.

The most popular antojitos – enchiladas, tacos, and tamales, are the mainstay of Mexican and Tex Mex restaurants around the world, but only a small part of the wide variety of Mexican cuisine on offer in most Mexican households.

HERE IS A LIST OF THE MOST POPULAR SAUCES SERVED WITH ANTOJITOS.

Red Chilli Sauce ➤ **p8**

Green Chilli Sauce ➤ **p8**

Fresh Red Tomato and Chilli Sauce ➤ **p9**

Fresh Green Chilli Sauce ➤ **p9**

Avocado Sauce ➤**p10**

Ranch Style Chilli Sauce ➤ **p10**

Red Enchilada Sauce ➤ **p10**

Cheese Sauce ➤ **p10**

Green Enchilada Sauce ➤ **p11**

National Tacos

Cheesy Turnovers

NATIONAL TACOS
TACOS DE POLLO NACIONALES

≈ TACOS

Traditionally, a taco is a heated tortilla folded over a bit of filling Tortillas can be warmed to soften them and be folded over the filling or deep fried into a taco shell (buy them readymade) with various fillings placed inside.

These tacos resemble the Mexican flag in colours of green, white and red.

12 soft tortillas

vegetable oil for cooking

1 green capsicum (pepper), cut into thin strips

1 cup (250 ml) sour cream

FILLING

2 cups minced cooked chicken, or 2 chicken breast fillets, cooked and minced

⅓ cup (80 g) cream cheese

3 tablespoons blanched almonds, chopped

RED CHILLI SAUCE

1½ tablespoons olive oil

1 spring onion, finely chopped

3 to 4 fresh or canned hot red chillies, seeded and finely chopped

1 clove garlic, crushed

3 tablespoons tomato purée

1 TO MAKE FILLING: Combine chicken, cheese and almonds and mix well. Season to taste with freshly ground black pepper and salt.

2 TO MAKE SAUCE: Heat olive oil in a saucepan and cook onion, chillies and garlic over a medium heat for 3 to 4 minutes or until onion is soft. Add tomato purée and simmer for a further 1 to 2 minutes.

3 Heat vegetable oil in a saucepan and cook tortillas until softened. Spread each one with a spoonful of chicken mixture, roll up and secure with toothpick.

4 Top each taco with a strip of green capsicum, and a band of sour cream and Red Chilli Sauce before serving.

NOTE: Prepared taco shells may be substituted for the tortillas in this recipe if you wish.

MAKES 12

WHEAT FLOUR TORTILLAS
TORTILLAS DE HARINA

2 cups (250 g) plain flour, sifted

½ teaspoon salt

60 g margarine or butter

⅓ to ⅔ cup (80 to 160 ml) warm water

1 tablespoon vegetable oil

1 Combine flour and salt in a mixing bowl. Rub in margarine with fingertips until mixture resembles coarse breadcrumbs.

2 Add enough water to mixture to form a soft dough. Knead lightly on a floured surface until smooth.

3 Divide dough into 12 equal portions and shape into balls.

4 Brush each portion with oil to coat and place in a bowl. Cover with a dry cloth and allow to stand for 15 minutes.

5 Roll out dough portions on a lightly floured surface to form tortillas about 20 cm in diameter.

6 Preheat a dry, heavy-based frypan over a medium heat. Cook tortillas for about 30 seconds each side or until speckled and cooked through.

7 Stack cooked tortillas in a basket or bowl lined with a cloth and cover to keep them warm and flexible.

MAKES 12

CHEESY TURNOVERS
QUESADILLAS

1 cup (125 g) dried masa or instant masa

½ cup (60 g) plain flour, sifted

½ teaspoon baking powder

¼ teaspoon salt

½ cup (125 ml) water

3 tablespoons milk

250 g mild Cheddar cheese, finely grated or 250 g cooked meat, bean or cheese mixture of your choice

12 fresh medium hot green chillies, trimmed steamed, seeded and chopped

oil for cooking

1 Combine masa, plain flour, baking powder and salt in a bowl. Combine water and milk. Add to masa mixture and mix to form a dough. Knead on a lightly floured surface until smooth.

2 Divide dough into 16 equal portions and shape into balls. Cover with plastic wrap or a damp tea towel.

3 Using a tortilla press, place a 22 cm square of plastic wrap or waxed paper over bottom plate. Place a portion of dough on top, a little off centre towards the hinge, and press with palm of hand to flatten a little. Cover with a second sheet of plastic wrap or waxed paper and close firmly, but not too hard. Remove tortilla from press and carefully peel away plastic.

4 Keep tortillas soft covered with a damp kitchen cloth until required.

5 Place a spoonful of cheese or meat cheese mixture on a tortilla and top with chilli. Fold tortilla in half and press edges together firmly with fingertips.

6 Cover with a damp cloth and repeat with remaining dough and filling.

7 Heat enough oil in a large saucepan to cover 3 cm deep, heat to 180°C (350°F) and cook quesadillas, a few at a time, until golden brown. Drain on absorbent paper. Serve hot with salsa of your choice.

MAKES 16

≈ **WHEAT FLOUR TORTILLAS**

The Mexicans in the north began making white-flour tortillas when the Spanish introduced wheat to Mexico. You can buy them readymade, fresh or frozen in Mexican food outlets, or you can make your own. They come in many sizes and are usually larger than corn tortillas. The larger tortillas are often used for making burritos.

≈ **TORTILLA PRESS**

Patting the dough into neat rounds by hand is not so easy, but by using a tortilla press, a small heavy cast-iron press, now available in most large Western cities, you can enjoy freshly made tortillas with a minimum of fuss.

≈ TORTILLAS

Enchiladas, tacos, tostados and totopos are all corn tortillas in some shape or form. No Mexican meal would be complete without tortillas. They are not only Mexico's daily bread, but they are the basis of a large number of everyday and fiesta dishes.

A tortilla can simply be warmed and served as a flexible bread to eat with a meal, or broken into soup croutons. It can be ground to thicken stews, soups and moles, or toasted then covered in a tasty topping and served as an appetiser, called a tostada.

CORN TORTILLAS
TORTILLAS DE MATZ

Like corn itself, corn tortillas have been part of the Mexican diet since ancient times. Their aroma as they arrive at the table is a heady one. You can buy ready-made corn tortillas from Mexican speciality food shops and restaurant suppliers.

Mexicans often use tortillas instead of spoons to scoop up their food from plates or bowls. In some villages, diners will even use tortillas as napkins to wipe hands and face after the last morsel of food is eaten and the final tortilla is then thrown away.

You will need prepared masa dough or as in the following recipe, dried instant masa cornmeal, which is widely available today.

2 cups (250 g) dried masa or instant masa
approximately 1⅓ cups (330 ml) water

1 Mix together masa and enough water to form a soft dough. Knead on a surface sprinkled lightly with extra masa until smooth and elastic.

2 Divide dough into 15 equal portions and shape into balls. Cover with plastic wrap or a damp kitchen cloth.

3 Roll out a portion to a 15 cm - 18 cm diameter between two pieces of waxed paper, or pat out by hand, to form a tortilla. Repeat with remaining portions.

4 TO MAKE TORTILLAS USING A TORTILLA PRESS: Place a 22 cm square piece of plastic wrap or waxed paper over bottom plate. Place a portion of dough on top, a little off centre towards the hinge, and press with palm of hand to flatten a little. Cover with a second sheet of plastic wrap or waxed paper and close, press firmly but not too hard. Remove tortilla from press and carefully peel away plastic.

5 Keep tortillas soft, covered with a damp kitchen cloth, until required.

6 Preheat a heavy-based frypan over a medium heat.

7 Cook tortillas for about 30 seconds each side or until speckled and cooked through. Stack cooked tortillas in a basket or bowl lined with a cloth and cover to keep them warm and flexible.

MAKES 15

TAMALES

250 g butter or margarine

5 cups (625 g) dried masa or instant masa

2 tablespoons baking powder

1 teaspoon salt

¾ cup (180 ml) chicken stock

25 corn husks or 8 x 10 cm parchment paper pieces

1 Beat the butter or margarine until light and fluffy. Combine the masa, baking powder and salt. Add stock and mix well. Add to margarine and continue to beat until creamy.
2 Soak corn husks in cold water for 1 hour to moisten. Pat dry with absorbent paper. Carefully flatten each one, and spread a large spoonful of masa dough over husk leaving a 2 cm border at each end.
3 Place filling of your choice, in a sausage shape, on top of spread masa dough and roll corn husks to enclose filling.
4 Pinch ends together and tie with a shred of corn husk or string to seal.
5 Stack tamales in a large steamer, being careful not to overcrowd, and cook gently over simmering water for 45 to 60 minutes or until cooked through.

MAKES 20 TAMALES

SAVOURY CHICKEN TAMALE FILLING
TAMALES DE POLLO

¼ cup (60 ml) olive or vegetable oil

¼ cup (30 g) plain flour

1 clove garlic, crushed

1 small onion, peeled and chopped

2 tablespoons tomato purée

1 teaspoon dried oregano

500 g cooked chicken, shredded

⅓ cup (60 g) blanched almonds

1 teaspoon chilli powder (optional)

1 Heat oil in a saucepan, stir in flour and cook over a medium heat, stirring constantly, until golden brown.
2 Add garlic, onion, tomato purée, and oregano, reduce heat and simmer for 15 minutes. Stir through chicken and cook for 15 minutes longer. Set aside and allow to cool. Use to fill tamales.

VARIATIONS: Use minced or shredded pork with raisins or cooked prawns or assorted seafood instead of the chicken and almonds and continue as above. Sweet corn also makes an interesting filling.

MAKES ENOUGH FOR 20 TAMALES

≈ TAMALES

Tamales are one of Mexico's oldest national snacks and are seen at every festive occasion. They were served at feasts for Montezuma and were an Aztec delicacy. They come in all shapes and sizes and differ from state to state. A tamale is similar to a stuffed dumpling. It is masa dough wrapped in a corn husk (or in banana leaves in the southern tropical areas of Mexico), filled and steamed. The fillings can be savoury or sweet. The savoury ones usually have a salsa or mole base and the sweet tamales, nuts or sweet sauces.

Tamales

SWEET TAMALES
TAMALES DULCES

1 cup (250 g) sugar

1 cup (110 g) ground nuts

½ cup (125 ml) milk

150 g butter

60 g margarine

2 teaspoons vanilla essence

1 teaspoon ground cinnamon

pinch ground cloves

pinch salt

1 teaspoon baking powder

4 cups (500 g) dried masa or instant masa

45 to 50 corn husks or 8 x 10 cm parchment
paper pieces

1 Combine sugar, nuts and milk and stir
until sugar dissolves. Set aside.

2 Cream butter and margarine until light
and fluffy. Beat in sugar mixture, vanilla,
cinnamon and cloves. Combine baking
powder and masa, add to butter mixture and
mix to form soft dough.

3 Soak corn husks in cold water for 1 hour
to moisten. Pat dry with absorbent paper.
Carefully flatten each one and spread dough
over husk leaving a 2 cm border at each end.
Roll corn husks to enclose dough. Pinch
ends together and tie with a shred of corn
husk or string to seal. Stack in a large
steamer, being careful not to overcrowd, and
cook over simmering water for 30 to 45
minutes or until cooked through.

MAKES 45 TO 50

TACOS WITH MINCED BEEF
TACOS CON CARNE MOLIDA

12 soft tortillas

2 tomatoes, peeled and finely chopped

1 small onion, peeled and finely chopped

1 cucumber, diced

125 g Cheddar cheese, grated

1 small lettuce, shredded

FILLING

½ tablespoon vegetable oil

500 g minced beef

1 small red capsicum (pepper), finely
chopped

1 onion, peeled and finely chopped

1 cup (250 g) drained canned tomatoes,
chopped

½ teaspoon sugar (optional)

2 tablespoons chilli powder

½ teaspoon ground cumin

pinch dried oregano

1 teaspoon dried coriander

1 Heat oil in a large heavy-based frypan and
cook meat over a medium high heat until
browned. Add capsicum and onion and cook
until onion is soft. Add tomatoes, sugar,
chilli powder, cumin, oregano and coriander.
Reduce heat and simmer for 10 minutes,
stirring occasionally. Season to taste with
freshly ground black pepper and salt.

2 Heat tortillas to soften in a dry, heavy-based
frypan over a medium high heat. Remove
from heat and spread a spoonful of meat
mixture over each tortilla. Top half tortilla
with tomatoes, onion, cucumber and grated
cheese. Fold tortillas in half to cover filling.

3 Place on serving plates and garnish with
shredded lettuce. Serve with Red Chilli Sauce.

MAKES 12

VARIATIONS: Substitute shredded cooked
chicken, refried beans or your favourite
vegetables

GREEN ENCHILADAS WITH PORK
ENCHILADAS VERDES CON PUERCO

SAUCE

3 tablespoons vegetable oil

3 spring onions, finely chopped

2 fresh, small, hot chillies, seeded and finely chopped

1 clove garlic, crushed

500 g canned tomatillos, drained and mashed

1 teaspoon dried oregano

⅓ cup (45 g) plain flour

2 cups (500 ml) chicken stock

1 cup (250 ml) milk

FILLING

1 kg lean pork, cut into 1 cm cubes

2 cloves garlic, crushed

1 onion, peeled and finely chopped

1 tomato, peeled, seeded and finely chopped

vegetable oil for cooking

12 soft tortillas

1 To MAKE SAUCE: Heat oil in a saucepan and cook onion and chillies over a medium heat for 3 to 4 minutes or until onion is soft. Add garlic, tomatillos and oregano and cook for 2 minutes longer. Reduce heat, add flour and cook for 3 minutes, stirring constantly. Combine stock and milk. Gradually blend into tomatillo mixture and cook over a medium heat, stirring constantly, until mixture boils and thickens. Reduce heat and simmer for 15 to 20 minutes longer, stirring occasionally.

2 To MAKE FILLING: Place pork and garlic in a large heavy-based saucepan and add enough water to cover. Bring to the boil, reduce heat and simmer gently for 45 minutes or until pork is tender, liquid has evaporated and the meat begins to brown. Add onion and tomato, cook for a further 5 to 8 minutes. Season to taste with freshly ground black pepper and salt.

3 Heat vegetable oil in a large saucepan and cook tortillas over a medium heat for 5 to 10 seconds or until the tortilla becomes limp and barely blistered. It is important that the tortillas are not overcooked. They should be still soft, not crisp. Remove and dip immediately in sauce.

4 Place a large spoonful of pork filling, in the centre of each tortilla and roll up to enclose. Arrange in a grease ovenproof dish. Spoon over remaining sauce and bake at 180°C (350°F) for 15 minutes or until heated through.

SERVES 4 TO 6

BEEF ENCHILADAS
ENCHILADAS CON CARNE

vegetable oil for cooking

12 soft tortillas

2 cups (500 ml) Red Enchilada Sauce

2 cups (500 g) Shredded Beef

500 g Cheddar cheese, grated

1 onion, peeled and finely chopped

1 Heat vegetable oil in a large saucepan and cook tortillas over a medium heat for 5 to 10 seconds or until the tortilla becomes limp and barely blistered. It is important that the tortillas are not overcooked. They should be still soft, not crisp. Remove and dip immediately in Red Enchilada Sauce.

2 Place a large spoonful shredded beef in the centre of each tortilla.

3 Sprinkle with cheese and onion.

4 Roll up tortilla to enclose filling. Arrange and place with the seam side down in a greased ovenproof dish.

5 Spoon over remaining sauce and sprinkle with any remaining cheese. Bake at 180°C (350°F) for 15 to 20 minutes or until heated through. Serve with lettuce, avocado, cucumber, onion, sour cream and lime.

SERVES 4 TO 6

VARIATION: use the filling of your choice, eg refried beans, chicken

≈ **ENCHILADAS**

Enchiladas were first made by the Indians in southern Mexico using a corn tortilla. In the northern state of Sonora they developed a white flour enchilada after the Spanish introduced wheat to the region.

In Mexico, enchiladas are usually dipped in a chilli sauce then fried and served immediately, but Western cooks have found it less messy to fry them first, then to dip them in sauce and bake them.

The basic ingredients for enchiladas are tortillas, filling, enchilada sauce and garnishes for the topping.

CRAB ENCHILADAS
ENCHILADAS DE JAIBA

vegetable oil for cooking

12 soft tortillas

2 cups (500 ml) Green Chilli Sauce

2 cups (500 g) crabmeat

500 g mild Cheddar cheese, grated

4 spring onions, chopped

2 tablespoons chopped fresh coriander

1 cup (250 ml) sour cream

1 Heat vegetable oil in a large saucepan and cook tortillas over a medium heat for 5 to 10 seconds or until the tortilla becomes limp and barely blistered. It is important that the tortillas are not overcooked. They should be still soft, not crisp. Remove and dip immediately in Green Chilli Sauce.

2 Place a large spoonful of crabmeat in the centre of each tortilla. Sprinkle with cheese and onions.

3 Roll up to enclose filling. Arrange in a greased ovenproof dish.

4 Spoon over remaining sauce and and sprinkle with any remaining cheese. Bake 180°C (350°F) for 15 minutes or until heated through. Serve sprinkled with coriander and accompanied with a side bowl of sour cream.

DRY TORTILLA SOUP
SOPA SECA DE TORTILLAS

3 tablespoons vegetable oil

12 soft corn tortillas, cut in to strips

50 g butter

1 onion, peeled and finely chopped

4 canned hot green chillies or steamed fresh
green chillies, finely chopped

1 cup (250 ml) cream

4 canned tomatoes, drained and puréed

pinch sugar

250 g Cheddar cheese, grated

1 Heat oil in a frypan and cook tortilla strips over a medium heat until crisp and lightly golden. Drain on absorbent paper.

2 Melt butter in a saucepan and cook onion and chillies over a medium heat for 3 to 4 minutes or until onion is soft. Add cream, tomato purée and sugar, reduce heat and simmer for 10 minutes. Season to taste with freshly ground black pepper and salt.

3 Cover the base of a greased 8-cup (2-litre) ovenproof dish with half the tortilla strips. Spoon over half sauce and sprinkle with half the cheese.

4 Repeat with remaining tortilla strips, sauce and cheese.

5 Bake at 180°C (350°F) for 20 to 30 minutes or until cooked through.

SERVES 6

STEP-BY-STEP TECHNIQUES

TORTILLA FLUTES
FLAUTAS

2 tablespoons olive oil

1 small onion, peeled and finely chopped

1 garlic clove, crushed

1 teaspoon ground cumin

¼ teaspoon chilli powder

500 g cooked minced chicken

1 tablepoon finely chopped fresh coriander

vegetable oil for cooking

12 soft flour or corn tortillas

Red or Green Chilli Sauce

1 avocado, stoned, peeled and sliced

1 Heat olive oil in a frypan and cook onion and garlic over a medium heat for 2 to 3 minutes or until onion is just tender but not soft. Add chilli powder and cumin and cook for 1 minute.

2 Stir through chicken. Cook over medium high heat until just heated through. Mix in coriander, remove from heat and set aside.

3 Soften tortillas, one at a time, by heating in a dry heavy-based frypan over a high heat for about 30 seconds each side or dipping in hot oil.

4 Lay tortilla flat and place a large spoonful of chicken mixture along centre of tortilla. Carefully roll the tortilla to form a flute.

5 Heat enough oil in a deep frypan to cover 5 cm deep. Holding the flute together with tongs (or fasten with toothpicks) cook in hot oil until slightly crisp. Drain on absorbent paper. Repeat with remaining tortillas and filling.

6 Serve with Red or Green Chilli Sauce and avocado slices.

SERVES 6

VARIATION: Use two tortillas, overlapping to make extra long, thin flutes

Place a spoonful of mixture along centre of tortilla, and carefully roll tortilla into a flute

Holding the flute together with tongs, fry in hot oil until slightly crisp

*Flauta is the Spanish word for flute.
These tacos are flute shaped – tubular with a delicious
filling and fried until crisp and golden.
Serve with your favourite chilli sauce.*

PESCADOS

FISH AND SHELLFISH

Mexico's coastline stretches thousands of kilometres with fishing grounds teeming with fish in the Pacific Ocean, the gulfs of California and Mexico, and the Caribbean. There are also estuaries and coastal lagoons with a rich harvest of prawns, clams and oysters.

The west coast in particular abounds with seafood. In Ensenada, even tacos are filled with lobster, prawns and fish nuggets, and in Mazatlan, fish stuffed with prawns and covered with freshly made mayonnaise is a speciality.

Ceviche, fresh, raw fish or shellfish marinated in lime juice, is served everywhere in Acapulco, and Veracruz is famous for its snapper. Huachinango Veracruz (Red Snapper Veracruz), is on every restaurant menu to be enjoyed at the colourful open air tables with lively Mexican music floating by on a sea breeze.

Seafood in Green Chilli Sauce

MAZATLAN SNAPPER
PESCADO MAZATLECO

Mazatlan offers some of the best fishing in Mexico. The ocean abounds with sailfish, red snapper, swordfish, tuna and many other seafoods.

Mazatlan Snapper

4 cups (1 litre) water

1 lime, thinly sliced

½ teaspoon dried tarragon

¼ teaspoon salt

2 spring onions, chopped

5 whole black peppercorns

3 whole cloves

pinch dried rosemary

pinch ground cinnamon

1 bay leaf

4 small red snapper

2½ tablespoons olive oil

1 small onion, peeled and finely chopped

1 clove garlic, crushed

3 canned tomatoes, drained and chopped

1 tablespoon chopped fresh parsley

3 tablespoons white wine

½ teaspoon ground coriander

1 fresh small red chilli, finely chopped

1 tablespoon dry cracker crumbs

1 cup (250 ml) Fresh Red Tomato and Chilli Sauce

1 Place water, lime, tarragon, salt, spring onions, peppercorns, cloves, rosemary, cinnamon, and bay leaf with snapper in a large saucepan and simmer gently for 5 minutes. Remove from heat and set aside.

2 Heat oil in a heavy-based frypan and cook onion and garlic over a medium heat for 3 to 4 minutes or until onion is soft. Add tomatoes and parsley and cook for 5 minutes longer. Stir through wine and coriander. Remove from heat.

3 Place fish in a greased baking dish and spoon over tomato mixture. Season to taste with freshly ground black pepper and salt. Sprinkle with chilli and cracker crumbs. Bake at 190°C (375°F) for 15 minutes or until fish flakes when tested with a fork.

4 Serve with Fresh Red Tomato and Chilli Sauce.

SERVES 4

GRANDMOTHER'S FISH IN LIME AND ROSEMARY
PESCADO ABULITA

2½ tablespoons chopped fresh rosemary

1 cup (250 ml) olive oil

1 cup (250 ml) fresh lime juice

1 clove garlic, crushed

2 fresh small red chillies, seeded and finely chopped

fresh coriander or parsley for garnish

1 kg sea perch or sea bass fillets, skin removed

1 Combine rosemary, oil, lime juice, garlic and chillies in a bowl. Season to taste with freshly ground black pepper and salt.

2 Arrange fish fillets in a ceramic dish and pour the marinade over them. Cover and allow to marinate in the refrigerator for 15 minutes.

3 Remove fish from marinade. Barbecue, grill or pan-fry the fish over a medium heat until fish flakes when tested with a fork.

SERVES 4

RAW FISH MARINATED IN LIME JUICE
CEVICHE DE JALISCO

1½ kg firm white fish fillets, cut into thin strips

1 cup (250 ml) fresh lime or lemon juice

2 to 3 fresh, small, green chillies, seeded and finely chopped (optional)

2 large tomatoes, peeled, seeded and finely diced

1 tablespoon finely chopped onion

3 tablespoons diced cucumber

½ teaspoon salt

pinch dried oregano

2 tablespoons finely chopped fresh coriander

1 Combine fish and lime juice in a bowl, cover and allow to marinate in the refrigerator for 2 hours or overnight, or until fish changes colour. Stir occasionally.

2 Drain some of the lime juice if mixture is too watery. Add chillies, tomatoes, onion, cucumber, salt and oregano and mix to combine.

3 Serve well-chilled, sprinkled with coriander and accompanied with lime wedges, avocado slices and a side bowl of chilli sauce and tortillas, if desired.

SERVES 4 TO 6

≈ **RAW FISH MARINATED IN LIME JUICE**

Fresh raw fish or shellfish prepared in this way is a very popular appetiser. It is 'cooked' by the acid in the lime or lemon juice, and looks and tastes as though it is poached. The fish is white and firm, losing its raw, translucent look. Ceviche is traditionally served with flat toasted tortillas, however, corn chips, nachos chips or dry crackers can also be used.

≈ **GRANDMOTHERS FISH IN LIME AND ROSEMARY**

Sharon's great grandmother Noble brought this very simple recipe for Pescado Abulita back from Mexico fifty years ago when she was living in a remote part of northern Mexico.

LOBSTER MARINATED IN ORANGE, LIME AND TEQUILA
CEVICHE DE LANGOSTA CON TEQUILA

1 kg raw lobster or crayfish meat, cut into serving pieces

2 cups (500 ml) fresh orange juice

2 cups (500 ml) fresh lime juice

½ cup (125 ml) tequila

6 spring onions, finely chopped

4 tablespoons chopped fresh coriander or dill

1 fresh small green chilli, seeded and finely chopped (optional)

1 Place lobster in a ceramic bowl. Combine orange and lime juices and tequila, pour over lobster meat and marinate in the refrigerator for 2 hours or overnight, or until lobster changes colour.

2 Add spring onions, coriander and chilli and season to taste with freshly ground black pepper and salt.

SERVES 4 TO 6

VARIATION: If you prefer, substitute 1 kg raw, peeled and de-veined prawns for the lobster

LOBSTER WITH RICE
LANGOSTA CON ARROZ

3 cloves garlic, peeled

⅓ cup (80 ml) olive oil

1 large onion, peeled and finely chopped

1 large green capsicum (pepper), chopped

500 g raw lobster or crayfish, cut into large pieces

¾ cup (185 ml) dry white wine

3 cups (750 ml) chicken stock

½ cup (125 ml) tomato purée

1 tablespoon sugar

½ teaspoon freshly ground black pepper

½ teaspoon dried oregano

½ teaspoon dried basil

2 cups (310 g) long grain white rice

90 g edam or mozzarella cheese, grated

1 Heat oil in a large heavy-based saucepan and cook garlic over a medium high heat until golden. Remove from oil and discard. Add onion and cook over a medium heat for 3 to 4 minutes or until soft.

2 Add capsicum and lobster and cook until lobster starts to change colour.

3 Stir in wine, stock, tomato purée, sugar, pepper, oregano and basil.

4 Bring to the boil, add rice and stir well. Reduce heat, cover and simmer gently for 15 to 20 minutes or until liquid is absorbed and rice is cooked.

5 Remove from heat and fluff rice with a fork. Sprinkle with cheese and cook under a preheated medium grill until cheese melts and turns golden.

SERVES 4 TO 6

FISH VERACRUZ
PESCADO VERACRUZ

This famous dish combines a cooked chilli, tomato and olive sauce with fish fillets. If you wish you can use a whole fish in place of the fish fillets and increase the cooking time by 10 to 15 minutes. Any fish can be prepared in this way – if you use Red Snapper you will have produced the famous Huachinango Veracruz.

3 tablespoons olive oil

1 medium onion, peeled and finely chopped

2 cloves garlic, crushed

2 fresh hot red chillies, seeded and finely chopped (optional)

4 large tomatoes, peeled, seeded and chopped

12 pitted or stuffed green olives, chopped

2 tablespoons capers

2 bay leaves

½ teaspoon dried oregano

½ teaspoon sugar (optional)

1 teaspoon cracked black pepper

1 kg red snapper, sea bass or similar fish fillets

½ teaspoon salt

2 tablespoons chopped fresh coriander or parsley

1 Heat oil in a large saucepan and cook onion, garlic and chillies over a medium heat for 3 to 4 minutes or until onion is soft. Add tomatoes, olives, capers, bay leaves, oregano, sugar and pepper. Bring to the boil, reduce heat and simmer gently, uncovered, for 10 minutes.

2 Place fish fillets in a greased shallow baking dish and sprinkle with salt. Spoon sauce over fish and cook at 180°C (350°F) for 10 to 15 minutes or until fish flakes when tested with a fork.

3 Sprinkle with coriander and serve with rice and warmed tortillas, if desired.

SERVES 4 TO 6

NOTE: This dish can also be cooked on top of the stove. Place fillets in a greased heavy-based frypan, sprinkle with salt and spoon over sauce. Simmer over a low heat for 8 to 10 minutes, or until fish flakes when tested with a fork, turning once.

Lobster in Tequila

This stunning seafood dish makes a wonderful centrepiece for a Mexican fiesta, or can be served as a meal in itself with fresh crusty bread or freshly warmed tortillas. You can make this dish two ways – as a Mexican style bouillabaise served in soup bowls, or using less stock, reducing to a thick sauce, and serving it as a seafood casserole with rice.

SEAFOOD IN GREEN CHILLI SAUCE
PESCADO Y MARISCOS EN SALSA VERDE

100 g white fish fillets, cut into small pieces

1 small cooked crab, jointed

500 g raw prawns

10 mussels, cleaned and bearded

10 small clams or scallops

STOCK

6 cups (1½ litres) water

2 red snapper heads

2 cups fresh prawn heads (optional)

1 cup (250 ml) dry white wine

4 carrots, peeled and quartered

1 leek, washed, cut lengthways and quartered

1 onion, peeled and quartered

1 turnip, peeled and quartered (optional)

14 cloves garlic

small bunch fresh parsley, chopped

2 bay leaves

1 teaspoon black peppercorns

GREEN CHILLI SAUCE

6 poblano chillies, (if unavailable substitute 4 fresh large hot green chillies and 2 medium, green capsicums (peppers), seeded and chopped)

1 large onion, peeled and chopped

small bunch fresh parsley, chopped

small bunch fresh coriander, chopped

4 cloves garlic

⅓ cup (80 ml) Green Chilli Sauce

1 TO MAKE STOCK: Place water, fish and prawn heads, wine, carrots, leeks, onion, turnip, garlic, parsley, bay leaves and pepper in a large saucepan or stock pot and simmer, uncovered, over a low heat for 1 hour. Strain into a bowl, reserving vegetables and discarding heads. Set aside and allow to cool.

2 Place ¾ cup (180 ml) cooled stock and vegetables in a food processor or blender and process until smooth. Return purée to remaining strained stock, stir and set aside.

3 TO MAKE SAUCE: Place chillies, onion, parsley, coriander, garlic and 1 cup (250 ml) cooled fish stock mixture in a food processor and blend until well combined.

4 Place blended ingredients and chilli sauce in a large heavy-based saucepan and cook over a medium heat for 2 to 3 minutes to release flavours. Add 2 cups (500 ml) remaining fish stock and simmer for 15 to 20 minutes or until sauce reaches desired consistency. (If you want you can add more blended parsley or coriander, chillies, or chilli sauce to strengthen the flavour.)

5 Add assorted seafood, cover and cook over a medium heat for 4 to 6 minutes or until mussels open and prawns change colour. Season to taste with freshly ground black pepper and salt.

SERVES 6

NOTE: A delicious soup can be made from the base of this dish by simply adding more of the stock before adding the seafood.

SOUSED OYSTERS
OSTIONES EN ESCABECHE

24 large fresh oysters in half shell

⅓ cup (80 ml) fresh lemon juice

⅓ cup (80 ml) fresh lime juice

1 tablespoon orange juice

½ teaspoon dried oregano

sprig fresh marjoram, finely chopped or ¼ teaspoon dried marjoram

3 black peppercorns

2 cloves garlic

1 bay leaf

⅓ cup (80 ml) olive oil

⅓ cup (80 ml) dry white wine

6 canned small chillies, finely chopped, or 6 fresh small chillies, steamed and finely chopped

1 onion, peeled and finely chopped

1 tablespoon chopped fresh parsley

1 tablespoon chopped fresh coriander

crushed ice

1 Remove the oysters from their shells and set aside. Clean shells and and reserve.
2 Place lemon, lime and orange juices, oregano, marjoram, peppercorns and garlic in a saucepan and gently bring to the boil. Remove from heat immediately and cool slightly.
3 Heat oil in a frypan and lightly sauté oysters. Drain on absorbent paper.
4 Combine wine, chillies and onion in a bowl. Add warm lemon and lime mixture and oysters, and stir gently. Cover and allow to marinate in the refrigerator for 3 hours or overnight.
5 **To Serve:** Spoon oyster mixture into reserved shells, sprinkle with parsley and coriander and place shells on a bed of crushed ice.

Serves 4

CODFISH MEXICANO
BACALAO MEXICANO

500 g codfish fillets

2 cups (500 ml) water

3 eggs

vegetable oil for cooking

1 kg tomatoes, peeled, seeded and roughly chopped

2 onions, peeled and roughly chopped

15 cloves garlic, crushed

2 tablespoons olive oil

100 g raisins

100 g blanched almonds

100 g pitted green olives, chopped

500 g baby new potatoes, cooked and quartered

1 green capsicum (pepper), cut into strips

3 fresh birdseye chillies, seeded and finely chopped

1 avocado, stoned, peeled and sliced

1 Place codfish and water in a bowl and allow to soak in the refrigerator overnight.
2 Remove fish and drain on absorbent paper. Cut into 2 x 8 cm strips.

3 Beat eggs until creamy. Heat enough vegetable oil in a large frypan to cover base by 2 cm. Dip fish pieces in egg mixture and cook in hot oil until golden and cooked through. Remove, drain on absorbent paper and set aside to keep warm.
4 Place tomatoes, onions and garlic in a food processor or blender and process until smooth. Heat olive oil in a frypan and cook until sauce thickens.
5 Add raisins, almonds, olives, potatoes, capsicum and chillies and cook for 3 to 4 minutes or until sauce is heated through.
6 Place fish on a warmed serving plate, spoon over sauce and garnish with avocado slices.

Serves 6   *Soused Oysters*

CARNE ∼

MEAT DISHES

The Aztecs, Mayans and other early civilisations of Mexico had very sophisticated cuisines long before the arrival of Cortez. They relied on seafood, game meat, fowl and beans for their protein.

The Spaniards brought farm animals to Mexico and so beef, pork, lamb and veal were introduced into the local cuisine. The Mexicans enjoy barbecued meats, especially beef and lamb, though their traditional barbacoa is to dig a big pit, wrap a side of beef or lamb in maguey cactus leaves, and roast it in the ground for eight hours. At every village market you can buy freshly barbecued meat, served in a folded tortilla and lathered in a hot salsa.

Many meat dishes are economical, using cheaper meat cuts and stewing or casseroling them with beans, vegetables or rich sauces to make them go further.

Steak Fajitas

GREEN CHILLI STEW
CHILE VERDE

3 tablespoons vegetable oil

1½ kg round or chuck steak, cut into
2½ cm cubes

2 green capsicums (peppers), cut into
2½ cm pieces

2 cloves garlic, crushed

440 g canned tomatoes, undrained
and mashed

200 g canned hot green chillies, seeded and
finely chopped or 4 to 6 fresh small green
chillies, steamed, seeded and finely chopped

small bunch finely chopped fresh parsley

2 tablespoons finely chopped fresh coriander

½ teaspoon sugar

pinch ground cloves

2 teaspoons ground cumin

3 tablespoons lemon juice or ½ cup (125 ml)
white wine

¾ cup (180 ml) beef stock

1 Heat 2 tablespoons oil in a large heavy-
based frypan and cook meat in batches over a
medium heat until browned. Drain on
absorbent paper.

2 Heat remaining oil in pan and cook
capsicum and garlic over a medium heat
for 3 to 4 minutes or until capsicum
is tender.

3 In a large heavy-based saucepan combine
tomatoes, chillies, parsley, coriander, cloves,
cumin, lemon juice and stock. Bring to the
boil, reduce heat and add meat and capsicum
mixture. Cover and simmer gently for 1½ to
2 hours, stirring occasionally.

4 Uncover and simmer for 45 minutes
longer or until sauce is reduced to a thick
gravy and the meat is tender.

NOTE: Pork, or a mixture of pork and beef,
may be substituted in this dish.

SERVES 4

MEAT IN GREEN MOLE SAUCE
MOLE VERDE

400 g canned tomatillos, drained

2 cloves garlic, crushed

1 California chilli or any large, mild to
medium hot red chilli, roasted, peeled and
seeded, or 1 canned large California chilli

1 large onion, peeled, steamed until tender
and chopped

1 tablespoon white vinegar

500 g cooked pork, veal, chicken or turkey,
thinly sliced

200 g canned whole jalapeno chillies

1 cup (250 ml) sour cream

1 Place tamatillos, garlic, chillies, onion
and vinegar in a food processor or blender
and process until smooth.

2 Place meat in a large frypan, pour sauce
over. Bring to the boil, reduce heat, cover
and simmer for 5 to 8 minutes or until
heated through and well combined.

3 Arrange on a serving platter garnished
with jalapeno chillies. Serve with a side bowl
of sour cream.

SERVES 4

Green Chilli Stew

Adobo is a seasoning based on dried red chillies and spices. The seasoning is rubbed in to the meat, and works like a marinade. You then barbecue or grill the meat under a fierce heat. In many Mexican markets you can see this vibrant red sliced beef, side by side with whole carcasses of beef, lamb, and pork. Here is a very simple recipe for pork adobo.

BEEF FILLETS IN CHIPOTLE CHILLI
FILETE AL CHILE CHIPOTLE

⅓ cup (80 ml) olive oil

4 fillet steaks

¾ cup (180 ml) beef stock or broth

20 g butter

4 corn tortillas

60 g edam cheese, grated

2 tablespoons chopped fresh coriander

CHIPOTLE SAUCE

⅓ cup (80 ml) olive oil

200 g canned chipotle chilles, drained or 2 dried chipotle chillies

1 medium onion, peeled and chopped

2 cloves garlic, crushed

½ green capsicum (pepper), chopped

500 g canned tomatillos, drained

4 tablespoons finely chopped fresh coriander

1 TO MAKE SAUCE: heat oil in a large frypan. Cook chillies over a medium heat for 3 to 4 minutes. Remove and drain on absorbent paper.
2 Add onion and garlic to pan and cook for 5 to 6 minutes or until onion is golden. Add capsicum and tomatillos and simmer for a further 3 minutes. Transfer mixture to a food processor or blender and process until smooth. Return purée to pan and simmer over a low heat for 20 minutes, gradually adding stock to retain sauce consistency.
3 Heat oil in a large heavy-based frypan and cook steaks over a medium high heat for 3 to 4 minutes each side or until browned. Add sauce to pan and heat gently for 5 minutes.
4 Place a steak on each of the tortillas. Sprinkle with cheese and place under a preheated grill until melted. Place on serving plates, pour hot sauce over each steak and sprinkle with coriander. Serve with extra warmed tortillas, rice and salad, if desired.

SERVES 4

NOTE: Two dried red chillies and 1 teaspoon paprika can be substituted if the chipotle chillies are unavailable.

PORK IN ADOBO MARINADE
PUERCO CON ADOBO

10 ancho chillies or 6 dried large hot chillies, seeded and crushed

1 cup (250 ml) vinegar

½ teaspoon dried oregano

4 cloves garlic, crushed

1 kg pork fillet, thinly sliced

1 Place chillies, vinegar, oregano and garlic in a bowl and mix to combine.
2 Place pork slices in a shallow ceramic dish, pour over chilli mixture and cover with plastic wrap. Set aside and allow to marinate for 2 hours.
3 Barbecue or grill pork over a high heat for 3 to 5 minutes or until cooked to your liking.
4 Serve with fresh tortillas and slices of cucumber, tomato and onion, if desired.

SERVES 4

BAKED PORK RIBS
COSTILLITAS DE CERDO AL HORNO

1 kg pork ribs

salt

2½ tablespoons adobo paste

1 cup (250 ml) fresh orange juice

1 tablespoon oil

2 limes, sliced

1 Season ribs with the salt and place in a shallow ceramic dish.
2 Combine adobo paste with ½ cup (125 ml) orange juice. Pour over ribs, set aside and allow to marinate for 1 hour.
3 Heat oil in a large heavy-based frypan and cook ribs over a medium high heat until browned on all sides.
4 Transfer to a greased baking pan. Pour over remaining orange juice and bake at 180°C (350°F) for 30 to 45 minutes or until pork is tender. Serve on a large platter garnished with lime slices.

SERVES 4

PORK LOIN IN BEER
LOMO DE PUERCO CON CERVEZA

1½ kg pork loin, boned

3 tablespoons olive oil

1 large onion, peeled and thinly sliced

1 tablespoon sugar

1 cup (250 m) beer

¾ cup (180 ml) water

4 apples or pears, peeled, cored and
thickly sliced

1 Trim most of the fat from the pork. Roll
pork and tie with string.

2 Heat 2 tablespoons oil in a large heavy-
based saucepan or stockpot and cook onion
over a medium heat for 3 to 4 minutes or until
onion is soft. Remove from pan and set aside.

3 Add pork to pan and cook until browned
on all sides. Return onions to pan. Dissolve
sugar in beer, pour over pork and simmer
until beer turns a dark golden colour. Add
water and simmer for 1¼ hours or until meat
is tender, adding more water if necessary.

4 Heat remaining oil in a frypan and sauté
apple slices over a medium heat for 1 to 2
minutes or until just tender.

5 Slice pork and arrange with apple on a
serving platter. Serve with vegetables of your
choice and rice or warmed tortillas, if desired.

SERVES 4 TO 6

SYLVIA'S PORK IN GREEN CHILLI SAUCE
PUERCO EN MOLE VERDE SYLVIA

1½ kg lean pork, cut into 2½ cm cubes

1 small onion, peeled and sliced

2 cloves garlic

pinch salt

water

2 cups (500 g) canned tomatillos, drained

5 serrano chillies or any fresh small chillies,
trimmed

1 tablespoon olive oil

2 tablespoons chopped fresh parsley

1 tablespoons chopped fresh coriander

CREDIT: PLATE, FORK AND SPOON – CORSO DE FORI

1 Place pork, onion, 1 garlic clove and salt
in a large heavy-based saucepan or stockpot
and add enough water to cover pork. Bring
to the boil, reduce heat and simmer, covered,
for 30 minutes. Remove meat and set aside.
Strain stock and reserve.

2 Place tomatillos, remaining garlic and
chillies in a food processor or blender and
process until a smooth paste forms.

3 Heat oil in a large heavy-based saucepan
and cook tomatillo paste over a medium heat
for 10 minutes or until thickened. Add 1 cup
(250 ml) reserved stock and bring to the boil.
Reduce heat, add meat and simmer gently for
1 hour or until meat is tender, adding a little
extra stock if necessary to produce the thick
gravy that typifies a mole sauce.

4 Serve garnished with parsley and
coriander, and accompanied with rice and
warm tortillas, if desired.

SERVES 6 TO 8

Pork Loin in Beer

Fajitas are traditionally tougher cuts of meat like beef skirt, marinated, and then barbecued over a high heat, quickly sliced across the grain and served. The results are tasty and tender as long as the meat is served immediately after it is cooked and sliced. Fajitas comes from the Spanish word faja meaning sash or belt, so skirt steak that comes from the midriff of the animal, in Mexico is known as fajita. Ready-made fajita marinades are available at delicatessens or Mexican restaurant suppliers. Fajitas are popular in Mexican restaurants around the world, and can be made with chicken, pork, veal or seafood. They go well with warmed tortillas and spicy salsas.

STEAK FAJITAS
FAJITAS DE CARNE

1 kg lean skirt or round steaks
1 tablespoon olive oil
small bunch fresh coriander, chopped
12 tortillas, warmed

SIDE DISHES
peeled and sliced Spanish onion
grated cheese
chopped radishes
chopped tomato
shredded lettuce
diced cucumber
yogurt or sour cream
guacamole
salsas

MARINADE
¾ cup (180 ml) fresh lime juice
6 cloves garlic, crushed
2 tablespoons Worcestershire sauce
⅓ cup (80 ml) tequila (optional)
3 tablespoons red wine
pinch dried oregano
pinch ground cumin
pinch sugar

1 To Make Marinade: combine lime juice, garlic, Worcestershire sauce, tequila, wine, oregano, cumin and sugar. Season to taste with freshly ground black pepper and salt. Place beef in a ceramic dish and pour over marinade. Cover with plastic wrap and set aside to marinate in the refrigerator for at least 1 hour, or overnight.

2 Heat oil in a heavy-based frypan and sear beef over a high heat for 3 to 4 minutes each side or until cooked to your liking, being careful not to overcook. (Alternatively, barbecue over a high heat.)

3 Slice meat thinly across the grain, sprinkle with coriander, and serve immediately either in the skillet in which it was cooked or on a warm serving plate. Allow people to help themselves to warmed soft tortillas to wrap the meat in, and a choice of side dishes.

SERVES 4 TO 6

VARIATION: Chicken, veal, pork and even fish or prawns can also be cooked in this way.

VEAL IN PEANUT SAUCE
TERNERA EN SALSA DE CACAHUATE

300 g unsalted blanched peanuts
4 tablespoons chopped fresh parsley
⅓ cup (80 ml) olive oil
1 kg veal, cut into 2½ cm cubes
2 cloves garlic, finely chopped
2 onions, peeled and finely chopped
2 large tomatoes, peeled, seeded and chopped
1 tablespoon sugar
pinch ground nutmeg
pinch dried oregano
pinch ground cumin
1¼ cups (310 ml) beef or chicken stock
¾ cup (180 ml) dry white wine

1 Place peanuts and parsley in a food processor or blender and process.

2 Heat oil in a heavy-based frypan and cook veal, garlic and onion over a medium high heat for 3 to 4 minutes or until veal is browned. Add tomatoes and sugar, bring to the boil, reduce heat and simmer for 5 to 10 minutes or until liquid evaporates.

3 Add peanut and parsley paste, nutmeg, oregano and cumin. Mix well.

4 Add stock and wine and simmer over a low heat, stirring frequently to prevent sauce from burning on the base of the pan, for 8 to 10 minutes or until meat is tender. You may need to add extra wine or stock if the sauce reduces too much during cooking.

SERVES 4

STEP-BY-STEP TECHNIQUES

MEXICAN SAUSAGE
CHORIZO ESPECIAL

1 ancho chilli or 2 dried small chillies, seeded and crushed

3 tablespoons vinegar

1 kg minced pork

1 onion, peeled and finely chopped

5 cloves garlic, finely chopped

2 bay leaves, crushed

3 tablespoons tomato purée

⅓ cup (85 g) finely chopped pimientos

1 teaspoon dried oregano

1 teaspoon ground cumin

300 g pork fat, finely diced

3 tablespoons tequila

sausage liner for eighteen 10 cm length, thick sausages

1 Soak crushed chillies in the vinegar for 10 minutes. Combine chilli mixture with remaining ingredients and mix well. Season with freshly ground black pepper and salt.

2 Gently stuff the mixture into the sausage liner, using a sausage stuffing machine or funnel, making sure not to overstuff as this will cause the sausages to burst during cooking. Twist the sausage every 10 cm to divide.

3 Hang sausages in a cool place or in the refrigerator for 2 days. Refrigerate or freeze until required.

MAKES ABOUT 18 SAUSAGES

SAUSAGE LINERS
Sausage liners – these are available from good butchers. If they are not already prepared, soak the linings for about 3 hours in warm water. Remove and rinse well. To help preserve the sausages, pour 1 cup (250 ml) vinegar through the linings and then drain before using.

CHORIZO
Chorizo is a hot and spicy Spanish sausage, to which the Mexicans have added spicy local ingredients. Usually red in colour, it is famous in mountainous Toluca, where it is sold in the markets to eat at breakfast, lunch and dinner. If you do not want to use sausage liners you can make the mixture into rissoles or sausage patties.

Combine chilli mixture with rest of ingredients

Gently stuff mixture in to the sausage liner

Twist the chorizos every 10 cm to divide

POLLO ~

CHICKEN AND POULTRY

Almost every family in rural Mexico has a small clutch of chickens. Even in the city, chickens can be found on the patios of tenement slums and in the courtyards of middle class neighbourhoods. Behind the traffic noise there is an incessant background symphony of clucking chickens and crowing roosters from the early hours of the morning.

Chicken is everyday fare, while turkeys and ducks are for special occasions or family celebrations. Wild fowl are popular in hunting regions like the eastern coast and also parts of Veracruz, where duck hunting is still a favourite pastime. Traditionally the Mexicans ate wild duck, turkey, pheasant, quail, pigeon and even turtledove, while the Spanish introduced them to domesticated poultry.

At fiesta time, the village landowners all contribute chickens for the communal feast in proportion to their property, and the chickens are barbecued, casseroled, steamed or fried and served with sauces or rolled in tortillas for enchiladas or tacos.

Green Spicy Chicken

CREDIT: PLATE – THE BAY TREE; SASH – CRAZY HORSE; KNIFE AND FORK – SHOP 2B CHELSEA HOUSE ANTIQUE CENTRE; TILES – COUNTRY FLOORS

MEXICAN COOKING CLASS 59

CLAYPOT CHICKEN
POLLO EN CUNETE

Mexicans cook this dish by sealing a cazuela (claypot) with masa dough or a paste of flour and water, and as the dish cooks bits of the paste break off and thicken the sauce. You can do this if you wish but it is not necessary.

1½ kg chicken pieces

6 to 8 garlic cloves, crushed

1 tablespoon coarse salt

1 teaspoon cracked black pepper

2 tablespoons vegetable oil

¾ cup (185 ml) red wine vinegar

2 tablespoons olive oil

2 teaspoons salt

6 bay leaves

1 tablespoon dried thyme

1 tablespoon dried marjoram

1½ cups (180 g) masa or plain flour, mixed with enough water to make a thick paste (optional)

2 fresh small red chillies

20 baby new potatoes, peeled

1 Rub chicken with garlic, salt and pepper to season. Cover and refrigerate for 2 hours.

2 Heat vegetable oil in a large heavy-based frypan and cook chicken until brown. Transfer chicken to a large heavy-based saucepan or casserole.

3 Add potatoes to pan in which the chicken was cooked and cook until lightly browned. Remove and set aside.

4 Add vinegar to pan and bring to the boil, stirring to lift sediment. Strain and spoon over chicken. Add olive oil, garlic, salt, bay leaves, thyme and marjoram to chicken and bring to the boil. Reduce heat and simmer for 5 minutes.

5 If using the paste cover chicken with mixture to seal and cook over a very low heat for 40 minutes, shaking the pot carefully every 10 minutes to prevent scorching the bottom of the pan. (Alternately, cover and simmer gently for 40 minutes, stirring occasionally.)

6 Unseal, add chillies and potatoes and season to taste with freshly ground black pepper. Simmer gently, uncovered, for 10 to 15 minutes longer or until potatoes are tender.

SERVES 6

GREEN SPICY CHICKEN
POLLO VERDE

1 tablespoon olive oil

1½ kg chicken pieces

100 g pork loin, chopped

50 g ham, cut into strips

1 onion, peeled and chopped

2 fresh small green chillies, finely chopped

4 to 6 lettuce leaves, roughly chopped

1 small bunch fresh parsley, roughly chopped

1 small bunch fresh coriander, roughly chopped (optional)

4 cups (1 litre) water

1 tablespoon vinegar

1 tablespoon plain flour

freshly ground black pepper

3 tablespoons capers (optional)

1 Heat oil in a large heavy-based pan and cook chicken, pork and ham over a medium high heat until chicken is browned. Remove and set aside. Retain 2 teaspoons of fat

2 Place onion, chillies, lettuce, parsley, coriander and 1 cup (250 ml) water in a food processor or blender and process until smooth. Transfer to a clean saucepan and simmer over a low heat for 5 minutes.

3 Add flour to saucepan in which the chicken was cooked and cook over a medium heat for 1 minute. Remove from heat and gradually blend in remaining water. Return to heat and bring to the boil gently over a medium heat, stirring constantly, until sauce thickens.

4 Add chicken mixture and purée. Season to taste with freshly ground black pepper and salt and simmer, uncovered, for 30 minutes or until chicken is cooked and sauce has reduced.

5 Serve with capers if desired.

SERVES 4 TO 6

Claypot Chicken

RED SPICY CHICKEN
PIPIAN ROJO CON POLLO

2 kg chicken pieces

3 cups (750 ml) water

pinch salt

6 ancho chillies or 3 dried medium chillies, trimmed

2 tomatoes, peeled and roughly chopped

1 teaspoon chilli powder (optional)

1 onion, peeled and sliced

2 cloves garlic, crushed

⅔ cup (100 g) sesame seeds, toasted

1 tablespoon olive oil

pinch ground cloves

pinch ground cinnamon

1 Place chicken, water and salt in large saucepan. Cook over medium heat until tender. Remove chicken, set aside. and reserve broth.

2 Lightly cook chillies in a dry pan over a medium heat for 1 to 2 minutes. Remove from pan and soak in warm water for 10 minutes. Drain.

3 Place chillies, tomatoes, chilli powder, onion, garlic and sesame seeds in a food processor or blender and process until smooth.

4 Heat oil in a heavy-based pan and cook paste over a medium heat for 1 to 2 minutes. Add cloves, cinnamon and chicken and 2 cups (500 ml) reserved broth. Reduce heat and simmer for 15 minutes or until sauce reaches desired consistency.

5 Serve with tortillas and salad, if desired.

SERVES 6

The state of Oaxaca is known as The Land of the Seven Moles. Each one is coloured by distinctive chillies of the region or in the case of the Green Oaxacan Mole, coloured by herbs. The dense moles or sauce dishes are better made the day before serving to allow the full flavours of chillies and spices to develop. In the black mole the colour comes from the dark dried chillies as well as the chocolate. We have tried to give substitutes for some of the chillies that are more difficult to find.

CHICKEN FAJITAS
FAJITAS DE POLLO

750 g lean chicken breast fillets

2 large onions, peeled, halved lengthways and cut into 1 cm strips

3 tablespoons olive oil

1½ cups (375 ml) guacamole

12 soft corn tortillas, warmed

1 cup (250 ml) sour cream or natural yogurt

2 tomatoes, peeled and diced

Tabasco or chilli sauce

1 tablespoon chopped fresh coriander or parsley

MARINADE

⅔ cup (160 ml) fresh lime juice

2 tablespoons olive oil

1 teaspoon dried oregano

½ teaspoon cracked black pepper

½ teaspoon salt

3 tablespoons tequila (optional)

1 TO MAKE MARINADE: combine lime juice, oil, oregano, pepper, salt and tequila.

2 Place chicken in a glass or enamel bowl, pour over marinade, cover and allow to stand in the refrigerator for 2 hours.

3 Place chicken breasts, marinade and onions in a greased baking dish. Cover pan with aluminium foil and bake at 180°C (350°F) for 15 to 20 minutes.

4 Remove chicken breasts and set aside.

5 Heat oil in a heavy-based pan and cook onion and remaining pan juices over a medium heat for 10 minutes, stirring frequently until onions are soft and golden brown. Drain excess liquid and transfer onion to a bowl.

6 Place chicken breasts under a preheated medium high grill or on a barbecue and cook for 2 minutes each side or until chicken is cooked through. Slice into 2 cm wide strips.

7 Place warmed tortillas on serving plates. Top each with chicken strips, onion, guacamole, sour cream, and tomatoes. Spoon over chilli sauce and sprinkle with coriander.

SERVES 4 TO 6

RED OAXACAN CHICKEN
POLLO EN MOLE COLORADITO

1½ kg chicken pieces

2 cups (500 ml) water

250 g ancho chillies or 50 g dried medium hot red chillies

6 guajillo chillies, seeded (if unavailable substitute 1 red capsicum (pepper), chopped and 2 teaspoons paprika)

440 g canned tomatoes, drained

1 onion, roasted

1 clove garlic, roasted

1 tablespoon sesame seeds, toasted

¼ teaspoon ground cinnamon

½ teaspoon dried oregano

60 g butter

50 g Mexican chocolate or bittersweet dark chocolate, melted

1 tablespoon sugar

1 Place chicken and water in a large saucepan and cook over a medium heat until tender.

2 Place chillies on an oven tray and cook at 160°C (325°F) for 10 minutes. Remove seeds and soak in warm water for 10 minutes. Drain and place chillies (or capsicum and paprika if chillies are unavailable) in a food processor or blender, with tomatoes, onion, garlic, sesame seeds, cinnamon and oregano and process until smooth.

3 Melt butter in a large heavy-based pan and cook the purée over a medium heat for 2 to 3 minutes. Reduce heat, add reserved chicken broth and chocolate and simmer for 10 to 15 minutes, stirring constantly, or until sauce thickens.

4 Add sugar and chicken pieces and simmer for 5 minutes longer or until heated through.

5 Season to taste with freshly ground black pepper and salt. Serve with tortillas, if desired.

SERVES 6

STEP-BY-STEP TECHNIQUES

BLACK OAXACAN MOLE

MOLE NEGRO DE OAXACA

1½ kg chicken pieces

3 cups (750 ml) water

50 g mulato chillies or any medium to hot very dark dried chilli, seeded

60 g guajillo or pasilla chillies (if unavailable substitute 1 teaspoon dark chilli powder)

60 g ancho chillies (optional)

50 g canned chipotle chillies, seeded

15 g butter

1 stick cinnamon

1 tablespoon blanched almonds

1 tablespoon roasted peanuts

1 tablespoon raisins

1 whole clove

2 cloves garlic

2 red capsicums (peppers), chopped

1 small onion, peeled and finely chopped

20 g butter or margarine

30 g Mexican chocolate or bittersweet dark chocolate

pinch sugar

2 tablespoons sesame seeds, toasted

Place mulato, guajillo and ancho chillies on oven tray and bake; cook chipotle chillies in a dry pan and then soak in warm water

1 Place chicken and water in a large saucepan. Cook over a medium heat until chicken is tender. Remove and set aside. Reserve broth.
2 Place mulato, guajillo and ancho chillies on an oven tray and cook at 190°C (375°F) for 5 minutes. Remove seeds and chop.
3 Cook chipotle chillies in a dry pan over a medium heat for 2 to 3 minutes, and then soak in warm water for 10 minutes. Drain.
4 Melt butter in a heavy-based pan and cook cinnamon, almonds, peanuts, raisins, cloves, garlic, capsicum and onion over a medium heat for 4 to 5 minutes or until capsicum and onion is soft. Transfer to a food processor or blender and process to form a smooth paste. Set aside.

Add chicken to chilli-chocolate mixture 10 minutes before end of cooking time

≈ CHOCOLATE

Mexican chocolate is available at Mexican food suppliers and specialty food stores.

5 Melt butter over a low heat in a small frypan. Add chocolate and melt, stirring constantly to prevent chocolate from burning. Add chilli paste and cook, stirring constantly, for 2 to 3 minutes. Stir through ½ cup (125 ml) reserved chicken broth to make a light gravy. Simmer for 30 minutes, stirring frequently, adding chicken 10 minutes before end of cooking. Add sugar and season to taste with freshly ground black pepper and salt.
6 Sprinkle with sesame seeds. Serve with warm tortillas and Mixed Salad Plate if desired

SERVES 6

CHICKEN WITH ORANGES
POLLO CON NARANJAS

2 kg chicken pieces

¼ teaspoon ground cinnamon

¼ teaspoon ground cloves

freshly ground black pepper and salt

3 tablespoons olive oil

3 cloves garlic

1 onion, peeled and chopped

1 cup (250 ml) fresh orange juice

1 cup (250 ml) water

½ teaspoon turmeric

2 tablespoons raisins

1 tablespoon capers

½ cup (60 g) almonds, coarsely chopped

3 oranges, peeled and segmented

1 Rub chicken with cinnamon, cloves and pepper and salt to season.
2 Heat oil in a large heavy-based saucepan or stockpot and cook chicken, garlic (whole) and onion over a medium heat until chicken is well browned on all sides.
3 Add orange juice, water, turmeric, raisins and capers. Cover, reduce heat and simmer for 35 to 40 minutes or until chicken is tender.
4 Remove whole garlic. Stir through almonds just before serving and garnish with orange segments.

SERVES 4 TO 6

CHICKEN IN GREEN PEPITA SAUCE
PIPIAN VERDE CON POLLO

1½ kg chicken pieces

3 cups (750 ml) chicken stock

6 fresh small green chillies, seeded and chopped

1 cup (220 g) canned tomatillos, drained

1 onion, peeled and chopped

2 cloves garlicf, peeled and chopped

1 small bunch fresh coriander, chopped

1 cup (85 g) pepitas, ground and sifted

2 tablespoons vegetable oil

1 Place chicken and stock in large saucepan and cook over medium heat until tender. Remove chicken and set aside. Reserve stock.
2 Place chillies, tamatillos, onion, garlic, coriander and ground pepitas in a food processor or blender and process until smooth.
3 Heat oil in heavy-based pan and cook puréet for 2 to 3 minutes. Stir through enough reserved stock to thin the sauce to the consistency of heavy cream. Season with black pepper and salt. Bring to the boil, stirring constantly. Reduce heat, add chicken and simmer, covered, stirring ocassionally, for 5 to 10 minutes or until heated through.
4 Serve with rice or tortillas and side dishes of guacamole and jalapeno chillies, if desired.

SERVES 4 TO 6

SPICY BAKED DUCK
PATO CON CHILE

1 x 1.8 kg duck

2 tablespoons chilli sauce

3 cloves garlic, crushed

1 tablespoon dried oregano

1 Combine chilli sauce, garlic and oregano well to make a thick sauce.
2 Spread sauce over duck and bake at 190°C (375°F) for 1 hour or until duck is well cooked. Baste with pan juices during cooking.
3 Carefully drain off the fat and serve the duck with tortillas and a tomato salsa.

CHICKEN BAKED IN PAPAYA
POLLO CON PAPAYA

1 x 1½ kg chicken

salt

1 onion, peeled and cut into eighths

2 cloves garlic, crushed

2 birdseye or seranno chillies, seeded and finely chopped

3 tablespoons chopped fresh coriander

1 large papaya or paw paw, peeled, seeded and cut into 1 cm wide slices

lime wedges for garnish

1 Rub inside of chicken with salt to season.

2 Combine onion, garlic, chillies and coriander in a bowl. Season to taste wih freshly ground black pepper. Spoon into chicken cavity. Wrap chicken completely with papaya strips. Place in a greased baking dish and bake at 180°C (350°F) for 1¼ hours or until chicken is cooked.

3 To Serve: Carefully unwrap papaya and remove stuffing. Cut chicken into serving portions. Mix stuffing with papaya. Arrange chicken and papaya mixture on a serving platter, garnish with lime wedges and serve with rice, if desired.

Serves 4 to 6

Spicy Baked Duck

ENSALADA

SALADS AND VEGETABLES

In Mexico, rather than serve vegetables as a dish in their own right, they are often disguised as part of a main meat or seafood dish. They could be creamed, fried or stuffed, or braised in a casserole and covered in a lavish sauce, as in the colourful Budin Azteca (Layered Aztec Casserole).

There is no shortage of salad vegetables either, but you are likely to find them garnishing another dish. Even a simple taco would not be complete without the stylish addition of some fresh tomato, lettuce, capsicum (pepper), onion and avocado. It was, after all, Mexico and the New World that gave us tomatoes and the chilli pepper, capsicums (peppers), avocado and corn, beans, zucchini (courgette) and many other varieties of squash. Even the potato came from the North American continent, though Mexicans prefer the camote or sweet potato.

Mexicans often mix fruit with salad vegetables. Avocado and papaya make a wonderful combination, especially when served with a dressing of freshly squeezed lime juice and olive oil.

Christmas Eve Salad

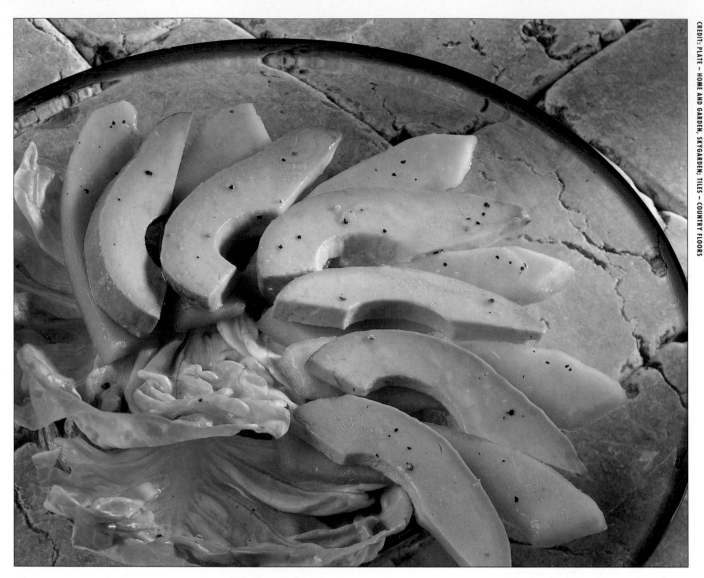

Avocado and Papaya Salad

≈ JICAMA

Jicama is a popular tuberous root vegetable that looks like a large yellow turnip. It has white meat and the taste of a bland, almost floury apple. Jicamas can be eaten raw with a few drops of lime juice and chilli powder, or can be fried, steamed or baked. It can be bought at Asian supermarkets, where it is called yam bean.

SAUTÉED BANANA CHILLIES

CHILES APLANADO

20 g butter

6 banana chillies or any mild large chilli, seeds removed and cut into strips lengthways

2 tablespoons fresh lime juice

1 Melt butter in a frypan and cook chillies over a high heat, stirring frequently, for 5 minutes or until chillies are tender.
2 Sprinkle with lime juice, season to taste with freshly ground black pepper and salt and serve warm.

SERVES 4

AVOCADO AND PAPAYA SALAD

ENSALADA DE AGUACATE Y PAPAYA

2 avocados, peeled, stoned and sliced

1 ripe papaya or pawpaw, peeled, seeded and sliced

1 small lettuce

DRESSING

⅓ cup (80 ml) fresh lime juice

⅓ cup (80 ml) olive oil

1 TO MAKE DRESSING: Combine lime juice and olive oil. Season to taste with freshly ground black pepper and whisk well.
2 Arrange avocado, papaya and lettuce leaves on four individual serving plates.
3 Pour over dressing and serve immediately.

SERVES 4

FRIED CHOKO IN LIME JUICE
CHAYOTES FRITOS

30 g butter

2 cloves garlic, crushed

2 large chokos, peeled, and cut into 1 cm slices

3 tablespoons fresh lime juice

1 tablespoon finely chopped fresh parsley

1 teaspoon finely chopped fresh chilli

½ teaspoon chilli powder (optional)

1 Melt butter in a large frypan and cook garlic over a medium heat until golden.

2 Add choko slices and cook, turning frequently, for 8 to 10 minutes or until golden brown.

3 Pour lime juice over the top and season with freshly ground black pepper and salt.

4 Sprinkle with parsley, fresh chilli and chilli powder.

SERVES 4 TO 6

LARGE CHILLIES IN WALNUT SAUCE
CHILES EN NOGADA

6 pablano chillies (if unavailable substitute banana chillies with insides rubbed with a small amount of chilli powder)

pinch salt

pinch ground cinnamon

1 cup (125 g) plain flour

3 eggs, separated

vegetable oil for cooking

FILLING

2 small tomatoes, peeled, seeded and chopped

1 small onion, peeled and chopped

1 clove garlic, crushed

30 g butter

1 plantain or 1 green banana, chopped

1 apple, cored, peeled and finely chopped

1 peach, stoned, peeled and finely chopped

1 pear, cored, peeled and finely chopped

250 kg cooked pork fillet, chopped

½ cup (80 g) blanched almonds

3 tablespoons raisins

1 tablespoon sugar

WALNUT SAUCE

1 cup (125 g) walnuts

1½ cups (375 ml) cream

sugar to taste

pinch salt

1 TO MAKE FILLING: Place tomatoes, onion and garlic in a food processor or blender and process until smooth.

2 Melt butter in a heavy-based frypan and cook plantain over a medium high heat for 4 to 5 minutes or until tender. Mash with a fork. Add tomato mixture, chopped fruits, pork pieces, almonds, raisins and sugar to pan and cook over a low heat, stirring occasionally, for 20 minutes.

3 Place chillies under a preheated hot grill and cook until the skin chars and blisters. Place in a sealed plastic bag for 10 minutes. Peel away skin, slit open and remove seeds and veins. Place in a saucepan with salt and cinnamon, cover with water and boil for 3 minutes. Drain

4 Fill each chilli with about 2 to 3 tablespoons of mixture, being careful not to overfill them. Overlap the edges to enclose the filling.

5 Roll each chilli in flour, coating lightly

6 Beat egg whites until stiff peaks form. Beat egg yolks with 1 tablespoon plain flour until thick and creamy. Fold gently into egg whites.

7 Heat enough oil in a large frypan to cover 2½ cm deep. Dip floured chillies into egg batter and cook in oil over a medium high heat for 3 to 4 minutes each side or until golden brown. Drain on absorbent paper, and set aside to keep warm.

8 TO MAKE SAUCE: Place walnuts, cream, sugar and salt in food processor or blender and process until smooth. Place in a saucepan and cook over a medium heat for 3 to 4 minutes or until heated through.

9 TO SERVE: Place chillies on a serving plate and spoon over walnut sauce.

SERVES 6

Alternatively you may like to bake the chillies. Place the Stuffed Chillies in a greased ovenproof dish, cover with a Ranch Style Chilli Sauce or Enchilada Sauce, sprinkled with grated Cheddar cheese, and bake at 180°C (360°F) for 20 minutes or until cooked through.

Pickled Chillies

PICKLED CHILLIES
CHILES ENCURTIDOS

Jalapeno or serrano chillies are ideal for this dish.

6 cups (1½ litres) water

1 cup (250 ml) vinegar

½ cup (125 ml) vegetable oil

5 bay leaves

2 tablespoons chopped fresh marjoram or ½ teaspoon dried marjoram

2 tablespoons chopped fresh thyme or ½ teaspoon dried thyme

1 tablespoon dried oregano

1 tablespoon cracked black pepper

2 onions, peeled and quartered

20 cloves garlic, peeled

½ kg fresh small red chillies

1 Combine water, vinegar, oil, herbs, pepper, onion, and garlic in a large heavy-based saucepan. Bring to the boil and add chillies. Boil rapidly for 2 minutes, then cover pot and remove from heat. Allow to stand overnight.

2 Spoon chillies into hot sterilised jars, cover with cooking liquid and seal. Store in a cool dark place.

MAKES ABOUT FIVE 1 CUP (250 ML) JARS

STUFFED CHILLIES
CHILES RELLENOS

8 canned or fresh Pablano chillies or 8 fresh banana or other large chillies (12 to 15 cm in length)

½ cup (60 g) plain flour

3 eggs, separated

1 teaspoon salt

vegetable oil for cooking

2 tablespoons chopped fresh coriander

chilli sauce of your choice

MEAT FILLING

1 tablespoon vegetable oil

2 tablespoons finely chopped onion

1 clove garlic, crushed

250 g minced beef

2 tomatoes, peeled, seeded and chopped

1 small bay leaf

5 almonds, chopped

1 tablespoon raisins

1 Drain canned chillies, rinse and make a slit vertically down the side of each. Remove the seeds and pith.

Prepare fresh chillies by placing under a preheated hot grill and cook until the skin chars and blisters. Place in a sealed plastic bag for 10 minutes to sweat off skin. Remove skin film by racking over the surface of chilli with a spoon. Slit open and carefully remove the seeds and veins, retaining the stems if possible.

If using a mild chilli like the banana chilli, rub the insides with chilli powder.

2 To Make Filling: Heat oil in a frypan and cook onion and garlic over a medium heat until onions are soft. Add beef and cook until browned. Add tomatoes and bay leaf, reduce heat and simmer for 15 minutes. Season to taste with freshly ground black pepper and salt. Mix in almonds and raisins and remove from heat. Set aside and allow to cool. Fill each chilli with 2 tablespoons of the filling, being careful not to overfill them. Overlap the edges to enclose the filling.

3 Roll each chilli in flour, coating lightly.

4 Beat the egg whites with salt until soft peaks form. In a separate bowl, beat egg yolks until thick and creamy. Fold gently into the egg whites.

5 Heat enough oil in a large frypan to cover 2 cm deep.

6 Dip floured chillies into egg batter and cook in oil over a medium high heat, for 4 to 5 minutes each side or until golden brown and cooked through. Remove and drain on absorbent paper.

7 Serve immediately sprinkled with coriander and accompanied by chilli sauce of your choice, and warmed tortillas if desired.

SERVES 4

Variations: Shredded Prawns may also be used as a filling for this dish.

SPINACH SALAD
ENSALADA DE ESPINACA

1 bunch spinach, stalks removed, washed and chilled for 1 hour

½ cup (125 ml) olive oil

30 g butter

4 spring onions, thinly sliced

4 to 8 fresh hot red chillies seeded and cut into thin strips

4 large tomatoes, sliced

250 g brie, sliced

1 tablespoon sesame seeds, toasted

DRESSING

1½ cups (375 ml) cider vinegar

2 teaspoons cracked black pepper

8 cloves garlic, crushed

2 bay leaves

½ teaspoon ground allspice

2 sprigs fresh thyme, chopped or ½ teaspoon dried thyme

1 To Make Dressing: Place ingredients in a screwtop jar and shake well. Stand at at room temperature for 1 day to allow flavour to develop.

2 Heat oil and butter in a large frypan and cook onion over a medium heat for 3 to 4 minutes or until soft. Add chillies and cook for 2 to 3 minutes longer or until onions are golden brown.

3 Arrange spinach leaves over a large platter. On one side of the platter place tomato slices and onion mixture alternately. Place cheese slices on the other side. Sprinkle with sesame seeds, pour dressing over and serve immediately.

SERVES 4 TO 6

PRICKLY PEAR SALAD
ENSALADA DE NOPALES

1 tablespoon olive oil

425 g canned nopales (prickly pear), drained and sliced

2 spring onions, finely chopped

1 clove garlic, crushed

2 large tomatoes, peeled and finely chopped

125 g Cheddar cheese, grated

2 tablespoons finely chopped coriander

pinch dried oregano

1 Heat oil in a heavy-based frypan and cook nopales, shallots, garlic and tomatoes over a medium heat for 5 minutes or until mixture is heated through. Season to taste with freshly ground black pepper and salt.

2 Place in a serving bowl and top with cheese, coriander and oregano.

SERVES 4 TO 6

≈ NOPALES

Nopales (paddles or pads) are tender cactus leaves and are sold fresh everywhere in Mexico. You can get the nopales or leaves canned or bottled in delicatessens. They are quite starchy when bottled and you should wash them before cooking. The simplest way to prepare the fresh fruit is to wash the pads with a stiff brush, or peel them with a kitchen peeler to remove the spines, then cut them into strips and again crosswise. Cook in water, covered, until tender. Drain, wash well, then season with freshly ground black pepper and salt. They are best sautéed with onions and tomatoes, or served with a vinaigrette or scrambled with egg.

LAYERED AZTEC CASSEROLE
BUDIN AZTECA

1 kg cauliflower, broken into florets

1 cup (250 ml) water

1 small clove garlic, chopped

2 medium egg tomatoes (Italian tomatoes), peeled, seeded and chopped

1 small onion, peeled and sliced

pinch dried oregano

250 g fresh negro chillies (or substitute 1 teaspoon turmeric, 1 teaspoon chilli powder and 250 g red capsicum (pepper))

8 tortillas, brushed with vegetable oil

250 g cooked chicken breast, chopped

250 g edam cheese, grated

½ cup (125 ml) cream

½ cup (125 ml) chicken stock, (mixed with the turmeric and chilli powder if not using chile negro)

1 tablespoon chopped fresh parsley

Layered Aztec Casserole

1 Place cauliflower, water, garlic, tomatoes and oregano in a large saucepan. Bring to the boil, reduce heat and simmer for 8 to 10 minutes or until cauliflower is tender.

2 Place chile negro or capsicum under a preheated hot grill and cook until charred and skin blisters. Place in a sealed plastic bag for 10 minutes. Peel, remove seeds and cut into thin strips.

3 In a greased ovenproof dish layer half the chile negro or capsicum, then 2 tortillas and half the cauliflower mixture. Top with 2 more tortillas, 125 g chicken, 125 g grated cheese, 3 tablespoons cream and 3 table-spoons stock. Repeat with remaining ingredients. Sprinkle with parsley and cook at 190°C (375°F) for 30 minutes or until golden brown.

SERVES 4

NOTE: You can also use dried chile negro reconstituted in water.

STUFFED PLANTAINS OR GREEN BANANAS
RELLENOS DE PLATANO

2 large plantains or 6 green bananas, cut into large cubes

1 egg, lightly beaten

3 tablespoons plain flour

¾ cup (185 g) refried beans

1¼ cups (310 ml) vegetable oil

⅔ cup (160 ml) sour cream

1 Place plantains or bananas in a saucepan with salted water. Bring to the boil and cook for 20 minutes or until tender. Strain and set aside to cool. Place in a food processor or blender and process until smooth.

2 Combine egg and flour, add plantain purée and mix well with hands to form a soft dough. Season with freshly ground black pepper.

3 Shape into twelve 6 cm patties. Place some refried beans on each pattie. Enclose beans in plantain mixture and reform patties.

4 Heat the oil in a large heavy-based frypan and cook patties for 3 to 4 minutes each side or until golden brown. Drain on absorbent paper.

5 Serve with sour cream.

MAKES 12 PATTIES

PRICKLY PEAR LEAVES IN SAVOURY SAUCE
SOPITA DE NOPALES

425 g canned nopales, drained and sliced thinly or 2 medium-sized fresh nopales paddles with spikes and spines removed

pinch salt

1 tomato, peeled, seeded and chopped

1 onion, peeled and finely chopped

1 clove garlic, crushed

water

pinch dried oregano

1 teaspoon chopped fresh coriander

1 tablespoon olive oil

2 eggs, lightly beaten

1 pasilla chilli, roasted, soaked in warm water for 15 minutes, seeded and chopped, or 1 dried red chilli, crushed

1 **TO PREPARE FRESH NOPALES:** Slice pads and boil until tender. Drain and peel away skin, being careful to remove any tiny spikes.

2 Place prepared nopales, salt, tomato, half onion and half garlic and water in saucepan, boil, reduce heat and simmer for 5 minutes.

3 Add remaining onion, garlic, oregano and coriander and season to taste with freshly ground black pepper.

4 Heat oil in a frypan, add egg and cook for 2 to 3 minutes, until cooked.

5 Slice egg into strips. Combine nopales, tomato mixture and egg in a serving dish and serve garnished with pasilla chilli.

SERVES 4

CHRISTMAS EVE SALAD
ENSALADA DE NOCHE BUENA

6 medium beetroots, peeled and sliced

250 g jicama or green apple, peeled and sliced

2 oranges, peeled and sliced

1 pineapple, peeled and sliced

1 red apple, peeled and sliced

2 bananas, peeled and sliced

½ cup (125 ml) fresh lime or lemon juice

1 lettuce

½ cup (155 g) unsalted roasted peanuts

3 tablespoons pine nuts

3 tablespoons pomegranate pulp (optional)

DRESSING

2 tablespoons sugar

¼ teaspoon salt

½ cup (125 ml) olive oil

3 tablespoons red or white wine vinegar

1 **TO MAKE DRESSING:** Combine sugar, salt, oil and vinegar and mix well.

2 Sprinkle fruits with lime juice while preparing them to prevent discolouration.

3 Line a large serving platter with lettuce and arrange fruits on top.

4 Sprinkle with peanuts, pine nuts and pomegranate pulp. Drizzle dressing over and serve.

SERVES 4 TO 6

≈ **CHRISTMAS EVE SALAD**

Ensalada de Nochebuena is one of the few salads served as a main dish in Mexican cuisine. On Christmas Eve families sit down together after midnight mass to eat the colourful and substantial beetroot and banana salad along with a turkey dish.

CREDIT: SERVING DISH – ALBI IMPORTS; TILES – FRED PAZOTTI

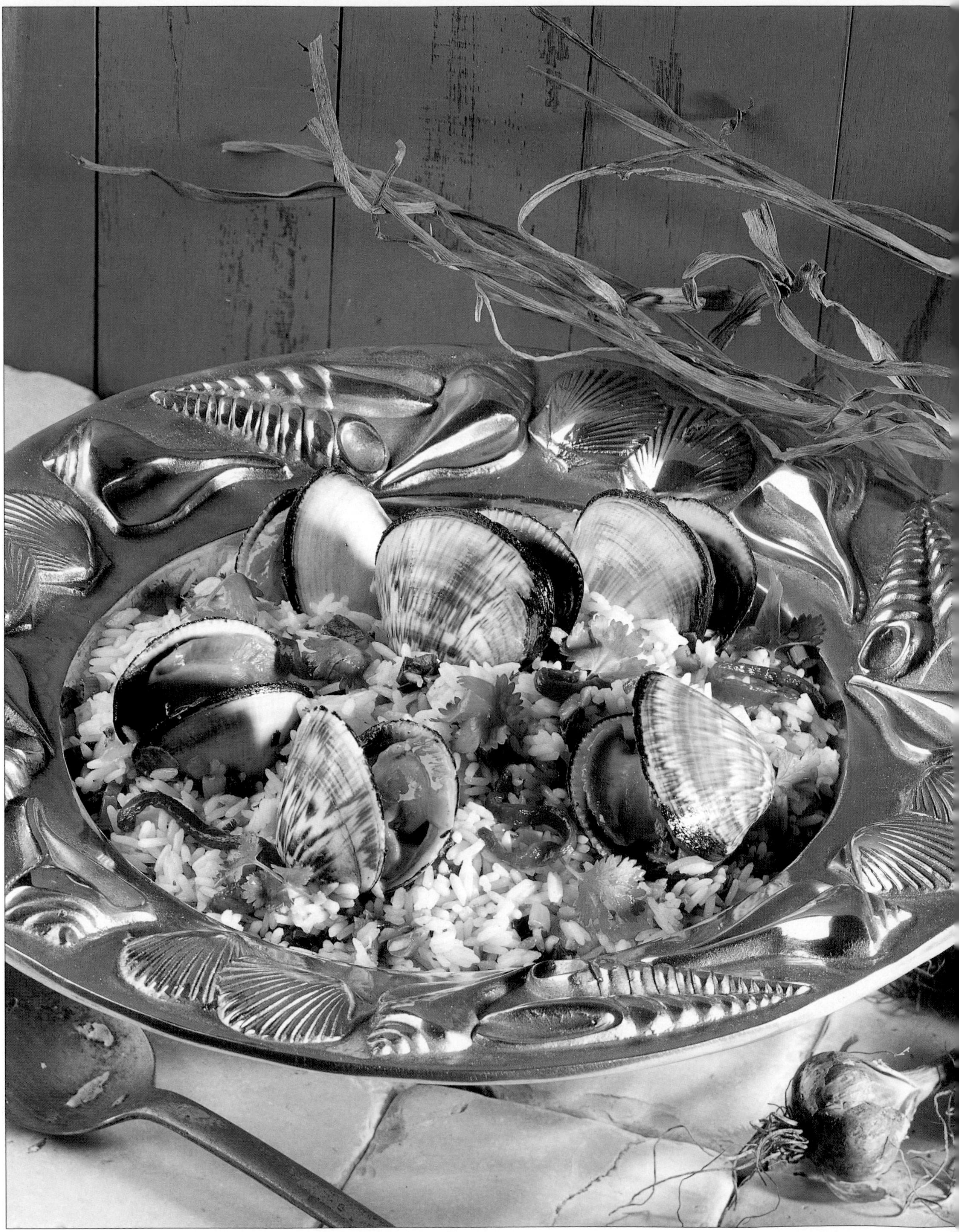

MAIZ
~

RICE, BEAN AND CORN DISHES

Though traditional Mexican meals include rice, bean and corn dishes, they are not necessarily served at the same time. Rice is usually served before the meat dishes, and beans follow a meat dish or are served on the side as an accompaniment.

Often rice dishes are confusing on a Mexican menu, as they can appear as sopas (soup). Mexicans regard many rice and noodle dishes as a dry soup, sopa seca, because it has absorbed lots of stock or broth.

Certainly both rice and bean dishes never reach a Mexican table unflavoured or unadorned. The rice is always cooked pilaf style, with some sort of vegetable, meat or stock for flavouring, and beans are usually mashed and fried, then served with a wealth of toppings.

Of course corn is on every table in the form of tortillas, but there are countless corn dishes, a few of which we have included.

Rice with Garlic Clams

BASIC BEANS
FRIJOLES SENCILLOS

2 cups (440 g) dried pinto, kidney or black beans

1 onion, peeled and finely chopped

2 cloves garlic, crushed

4 tablespoons olive oil

pinch salt

1 Place beans in a large ceramic or enamelled bowl and add enough hot water to cover. Allow to stand for at least 8 hours.

2 Drain, rinse and place in a heavy-based saucepan. Cover with hot water. Bring to the boil and add onion and garlic. Reduce heat and simmer gently, uncovered, for 2 hours, adding more boiling water when necessary to keep beans covered.

3 Add oil and salt. Continue to simmer, adding more water when necessary, for 2 to 3 hours longer or until beans are very tender.

SERVES 4 TO 6

MEXICAN WHITE RICE
ARROZ BLANCA

2 cups (310 g) long grain white rice

⅓ cup (80 ml) vegetable oil

⅓ cup (60 g) blanched almonds, toasted (optional)

pinch salt

4 cups (1 litre) hot chicken stock or broth

1 Rinse rice under cold running water until water runs clear. Set aside. Heat oil in a large heavy-based frypan, add rice and stir to coat with oil.

2 Sir in almonds and salt and cook over a medium heat, stirring constantly, until rice is golden. Pour over boiling stock and cover. Reduce heat and simmer gently for 15 to 20 minutes or until liquid is absorbed and rice is cooked.

3 Fluff rice with a fork before serving.

SERVES 4

TRADITIONAL REFRIED BEANS
FRIJOLES REFRITOS

45 g lard or bacon dripping

3 cups (660 g) Basic Beans

2 cups (500 ml) cooking liquid from Basic Beans

1 Heat lard in a large heavy-based frypan. Add well-drained beans, several spoonfuls at a time, with a little bean stock and mash with the back of a fork. Season to taste with freshly ground black pepper and salt.

2 Simmer and continue mashing to desired consistency, adding more stock if required. If you wish you can add chopped onion, dried chilli powder, sour cream or herbs to vary the flavour of this dish.

3 TO SERVE: Top with your choice of garnish. These could include sour cream or natural yogurt, sliced avocado, chopped onion, parsley or coriander, fried chorizo, fresh chilli finely chopped or capsicum (pepper), a salsa of your choice, or grated cheese.

SERVES 4 TO 6

VARIATION: A low fat way to prepare an alternative to refried beans is to simply put cooked beans in a food processor and roughly purée them. They will not have the same rich, full flavour, but they will certainly have fewer calories!

MEXICAN STYLE RICE
ARROZ MEXICANA

2 tablespoons olive oil

1 small onion, peeled and finely chopped

1 tomato, peeled and finely chopped

1½ cups (230 g) long grain white rice

3 cups (750 ml) chicken stock or broth

1 small carrot, peeled and diced

1 green capsicum (pepper), chopped

½ cup (50 g) fresh or frozen peas

1 lime, cut into wedges

1 Heat oil in a heavy-based saucepan and cook onion over a medium heat for 5 to 6 minutes or until golden. Add tomato and cook until tender.

2 Add rice and cook for 3 to 4 minutes, stirring constantly. Add stock, carrot, capsicum and fresh peas, reduce heat, cover and simmer gently for 15 to 20 minutes or until liquid is absorbed and rice is cooked. If using frozen peas, add 5 minutes before the end of cooking.

3 Serve with lime wedges.

SERVES 4 TO 6

CORN PUDDING
BUDIN DE ELOTE

3 tablespoons dried breadcrumbs

2 cups (340 g) canned corn kernels

½ cup (125 ml) milk

100 g butter

3 eggs

pinch sugar

1 cup (250 ml) Red Chilli Sauce

1 Grease a 1-litre soufflé dish and sprinkle with breadcrumbs.

2 Place corn and milk in a food processor or blender and process into a rough purée.

3 Beat butter until creamy. Gradually add corn purée and beat to combine. Add eggs one by one, beating well after each addition. Mix in sugar and season to taste with freshly ground black pepper and salt.

4 Pour the mixture into prepared dish and bake at 180°C (350°F) for 30 minutes or until golden brown and cooked through. Serve with Red Chilli Sauce.

SERVES 4

Corn Pudding

This is a dish that came to Mexico with the Spanish Basques and is a version of Paella. You can use any clam-like shellfish. Around the South Pacific, you can substitute the Australian eugari or New Zealand pippi.

RICE WITH GARLIC CLAMS
ARROZ CON ALMEJAS

24 fresh clams, unopened

1 cup cornmeal (polenta) or breadcrumbs

4 cups (1 litre) water

3 onions, peeled and finely chopped

¾ cup (185 ml) olive oil

1 large spring onion, chopped

3 cloves garlic, crushed

1 teaspoon paprika or chilli powder

1 fresh hot red chilli, finely chopped (optional)

4 tablespoons finely chopped fresh parsley

2 cups (310 g) long grain white rice

6 cups (1½ litres) fish or chicken stock

4 tablespoons chopped fresh coriander leaves

1 canned pimento, cut into thin strips

1 lime, cut into wedges

1 Place clams in a large bowl and cover with water. Sprinkle with cornmeal and allow to stand in the refrigerator overnight.

2 Drain clams and scrub clean. Place in a saucepan with water and half the onions and cook over a low heat until they open. Remove clams and set aside to keep warm. (Do not overcook them as they will become tough).

3 Heat ⅓ cup (80 ml) oil in a frypan and cook remaining onions, spring onion, 1½ cloves garlic, paprika, chilli and 2 tablespoons parsley over a medium heat for 2 to 3 minutes.

4 Combine rice, stock and onion mixture in a large heavy-based saucepan. Cover, and simmer gently for 15 to 20 minutes or until liquid is absorbed and rice is cooked.

5 Heat remaining oil and cook remaining garlic and parsley for 2 to 3 minutes.

5 TO SERVE: Arrange clams in their shells on a bed of rice and drizzle with hot garlic oil. Sprinkle with coriander leaves, garnish with strips of pimiento and serve with lime wedges. Serve with a hot chilli sauce and a salad, if desired.

SERVES 4 TO 6

BEANS AND PORK STEW
FRIJOLES CHARROS

3 rashers bacon, chopped

500 g pork, cut into 2 cm pieces

2 cups (500 ml) Red Chilli Sauce

100 g ancho chillies, crushed or 1 dark dried chilli, crushed and 1 small green capsicum (pepper), finely chopped

500 g pinto beans, soaked in 2 to 3 cups water overnight

2 cups (500 ml) beer

1 Cook bacon in a heavy-based frypan for 3 to 4 minutes. Remove from pan and drain on absorbent paper.

2 Add pork to pan and cook over a medium heat until browned. Add Red Chilli Sauce and chillies, reduce heat and simmer for 15 minutes.

3 Add bacon, beans with their water, and beer. Simmer for 2 to 3 hours or until the beans are tender. Serve with tortillas and rice.

SERVES 4

DRY RICE SOUP WITH PRAWNS
SOPA SECA DE ARROZ CON CAMARONES

½ cup (125 ml) vegetable oil

2 cups (310 g) long grain white rice

2 onions, peeled and finely chopped

2 cloves garlic, crushed

4 tomatoes, peeled, seeded and finely chopped or 440 g canned tomatoes, drained and chopped

4 cups (1 litre) chicken stock or prawn stock

2 fresh hot green chillies, seeded and finely chopped

400 g shelled cooked prawns, de-veined

2 tablespoons chopped fresh coriander

1 Heat oil in a heavy-based saucepan and cook rice over a medium heat for 3 to 4 minutes or until golden brown.

2 Add onion, garlic, and tomato and cook for a further 2 to 3 minutes. Add 3 cups (750 ml) stock and chillies. Cover, reduce heat and simmer gently for 25 to 30 minutes, adding extra stock if necessary during cooking or until liquid is absorbed and rice is cooked.

SERVES 4 TO 6

CHILE CON CARNE

3 tablespoons vegetable oil

1 kg lean minced beef

1 medium onion, peeled and chopped

1 green capsicum (pepper), chopped

1 clove garlic, crushed

3 to 4 fresh birdseye chillies, finely chopped (optional)

1 to 2 teaspoons chilli powder

1 teaspoon ground cumin

1 teaspoon paprika

½ teaspoon dried oregano

1 teaspoon sugar

1 bay leaf

440 g canned tomatoes, undrained and mashed

440 g canned kidney or pinto beans

2 cups (500 ml) beef stock

1 tablespoon plain flour, mixed to a smooth paste with 3 tablespoons water

1 tablespoon cornmeal (polenta)

1 Heat oil in a large heavy-based saucepan and cook minced beef, onion, capsicum and garlic over a medium high heat until meat is browned. Add fresh chillies, chilli powder, cumin, paprika, oregano, sugar, bay leaf, tomatoes stock and beans and stir over heat for 2 minutes to combine. Reduce heat and simmer 1 hour, stirring occasionally.

2 Add flour mixture and cornmeal and cook, stirring constantly, until thickened. Serve with rice and tortillas and sour cream if desired.

SERVES 4

≋ **DRY RICE SOUP WITH PRAWNS**

VARIATION: *Alternatively this dish can be cooked, covered, at 180°C (350°F) for 50 minutes or until liquid is absorbed and rice is cooked. Five minutes before the end of cooking, stir through prawns, cover and continue cooking. Just prior to serving, stir through coriander and season to taste with freshly ground black pepper and salt.*

Chile Con Carne

POSTRE

~

DESSERTS, MEXICAN COCKTAILS AND OTHER DRINKS

In a country where beauty is measured by the kilogram, Mexicans have no problem feasting on the most delectable desserts, cakes and drinks. Kilojoules and calories are just not an issue. And they love cocktails. Mexican drinks include tequila with its sharp bite, and the rich coffee liqueur, kahlua, both famous the world over.

Mexicans start the day with hot chocolate, progress through milky coffee (café con leche) or tea (té) and after the main meal of the day at lunch-time they will linger over strong, black, spicy sweet coffee (café de olla) before the afternoon siesta.

Mexican desserts and sweets range from the most exotic of tropical fruit mousses, ices, nut brittles, fudges and candies, to the famous flan – the golden caramel and egg custard the Mexicans gladly took from Spain and adopted as their own national dessert. Even today the flan vendor is one of the most popular figures in Mexico, with his almost melancholy call as he trudges the streets laden with colourful gelatinas and golden flans.

Oranges in Syrup

ROYAL EGGS
HUEVOS REALES

This is another Spanish dish that the Mexicans have embraced as their own.

8 egg yolks

2 egg whites

SYRUP

1½ cups (375 g) sugar

3 whole cloves

½ cup (125 ml) water

1 stick cinnamon

½ cup (60 g) pine nuts or slivered almonds

⅓ cup (90 g) raisins soaked in 3 tablespoons dark rum or brandy

1 Beat egg yolks until thick and creamy. Beat egg whites until stiff peaks form. Fold into beaten yolks. Pour into a well greased and lined 20 cm square cake pan. Place in a larger baking dish and add enough water to the baking dish to come halfway up the sides of the cake pan. Bake at 180°C (350°F) for 15 to 20 minutes or until well puffed and set. Remove and set aside to cool in cake pan.

2 TO MAKE SYRUP: Place sugar, cloves, water and cinnamon in a saucepan. Cook over a medium heat, stirring constantly until sugar dissolves. Bring to the boil and cook for 2 minutes. Remove cloves and cinnamon. Strain rum from raisins and add liquor to syrup. Set rasins aside.

3 When egg mixture is cool, cut into serving portions and place on individual serving plates. Pour hot syrup over cake and allow to stand until syrup is cold.

4 Serve sprinkled with nuts and raisins.

SERVES 6

MANGO CREAM
CREMA DE MANGO

This is a popular dessert in Mexico City. Substitute canned mangoes if fresh are unavailable.

3 large ripe mangoes, peeled, seeded and puréed

1 orange, pith removed, peeled and finely chopped

2 teaspoons fresh lemon or lime juice

3 tablespoons Cointreau, Triple Sec or similar orange liqueur

sugar

1 cup (250 ml) cream, whipped

½ cup (90 g) pecans, coarsely chopped

red glacé cherries

1 Combine mango purée, orange, lemon juice, liqueur and sugar to taste. Fold in cream and then pecans.

2 Spoon into parfait glasses and refrigerate until well chilled.

3 Serve garnished with cherries.

SERVES 4 TO 6

Royal Eggs

MEXICAN CUSTARD
FLAN

This dessert is a favourite. You can make individual flans or adjust the recipe for one large flan, which can be made in a mould or casserole.

4 cups (1 litre) milk

½ cup (125 g) sugar

½ teaspoon ground cinnamon

¼ teaspoon salt

1 teaspoon vanilla essence

1 tablespoon finely grated orange or lemon rind

2 eggs, lightly beaten

2 egg yolks, lightly beaten

½ cup (125 ml) dark rum (optional)

TOFFEE

¾ cup (180 g) sugar

⅓ cup (80 ml) water

1 To MAKE TOFFEE: Place sugar and water in a small heavy-based saucepan and cook over a low heat, stirring constantly, until sugar dissolves. Bring to the boil and cook, without stirring, until it reaches a golden colour. Pour a small amount into six greased individual ramekins to cover base. Set aside.

2 Place milk, sugar, cinnamon, salt, vanilla and orange rind in a saucepan and cook over a very low heat, stirring constantly until mixture boils. Simmer gently until milk has reduced to about 3 cups (750 ml). Set aside and cool to lukewarm.

3 Combine eggs and egg yolks and stir into milk mixture. Mix well. Strain custard through muslin or a fine sieve. Pour into prepared ramekins and place in a baking pan. Add enough hot water to the baking pan to come halfway up the sides of the ramekins.

4 Cook in the lowest part of the oven at 180°C (350°F) for 25 to 30 minutes or until a sharp knife inserted comes out clean. Remove from oven and allow to stand for 15 minutes. Remove from water bath and allow to cool completely and then chill for 2 to 3 hours.

5 To UNMOULD: carefully run a round-ended knife or spatula around the edge of the flans. Place a serving plate on top of the mould and invert. (If the caramel sticks, place the mould in a dish of hot water for a few seconds and then unmould.)

6 Warm rum and pour over flans just before serving. Ignite and serve flaming.

SERVES 6

NOTE: To make a larger flan pour custard into a prepared 6-cup (1½ litre) capacity ovenproof dish. Cook for 45 to 60 minutes or until a knife inserted comes out clean. Cooking time will depend on dish depth.

FOR COCONUT FLAN: substitute 1 cup (250 ml) coconut cream for 1 cup (250 ml) milk.

CANDIED LIMES
DULCE DE LIMONES

24 large limes

1½ cups (375 g) sugar

½ teaspoon salt

⅓ cup (80 ml) fresh lemon juice

¾ cup (180 ml) water

1 Scrape limes with a fork to mark surface, partially removing the the rind. Cut each one with a long vertical slit. Soak limes in cold water for three days, changing the water every 12 hours, squeezing the limes slightly as you do so.

2 Place sugar, salt, lemon juice and water in a heavy-based saucepan and cook over a medium heat, stirring constantly until sugar dissolves. Bring to the boil, reduce heat, add limes and simmer gently for 15 minutes. Remove from heat, set aside and allow limes to stand in syrup 8 hours.

3 Return to heat, bring to the boil and cook over a medium heat for 15 minutes. Remove from heat, set aside and allow lime to stand in syrup for 8 hours longer. Repeat cooking as above and simmer until limes are transparent.

MAKES 24

≈ **BAIN MARIE**

Mexican custard is cooked in a bain marie or as the Mexicans call it a bano da Maria, a larger pan containing hot water.

Mexican Puffed Fritters with Mexican Hot Chocolate

MEXICAN PUFFED FRITTERS
BUNUELOS

The recipe for Bunuelos originally came to Mexico from Spain. The Mexican variety is flatter, though still light and crisp. Bunuelos are eaten throughout the year but have a special place at Christmas when they are served with hot chocolate.

4 cups (500 g) plain flour

1 teaspoon baking powder

1 teaspoon salt

2 eggs, lightly beaten

1 cup (250 ml) milk

1 teaspoon ground aniseed (sweet cumin) boiled in ½ cup (125 ml) water, cooled and strained

vegetable oil for cooking

SYRUP

¾ cup (90 g) dark brown sugar

½ cup (125 ml) water

½ cup (125 ml) white wine

½ teaspoon ground cinnamon

1 teaspoon ground aniseed (sweet cumin) (optional)

1 TO MAKE SYRUP: Combine sugar, water, wine, cinnamon and aniseed in a saucepan. Bring to the boil and cook until a thick syrup forms.

2 Sift together flour, baking powder, and salt into a mixing bowl. Whisk together eggs and milk. Add aniseed water and sifted ingredients and mix to a soft dough. Turn on to a floured surface and knead well until smooth. Roll out half the dough as thinly as possible, until almost transparent, on a lightly floured surface and cut into 15 cm rounds using an upturned saucer. Repeat with remaining dough.

3 Heat oil in a large saucepan and cook Bunuelos for 30 to 40 seconds or until golden. Drain on absorbent paper.

4 TO SERVE: Break bunuelos into quarters. Divide quarters between individual shallow serving bowls and spoon over hot syrup.

SERVES 6

HOT CHOCOLATE
CHOCOLATE MEXICANO

For the best Mexican hot chocolate use the tablets or small cakes of Mexican chocolate.

3 cups (750 ml) milk

1 x 90 g tablet Mexican chocolate (or alternatively use 90 g semi-sweet dark chocolate, 2 tablespoons sugar, ½ teaspoon ground cinnamon and ¼ teaspoon vanilla essence)

1 Combine milk and chocolate (and sugar, cinnamon and vanilla if using) in a saucepan and bring to the boil, stirring constantly.

2 When chocolate is soft beat until well blended and the mixture stops boiling. Bring back to the boil and repeat beating as above.

3 Bring back to the boil again and beat a third time over the heat to make the mixture as frothy as possible.

4 Pour into cups and serve immediately.

SERVES 4

NOTE: Traditional Chocolate Mexicano is beaten with a molinillo (a wooden Mexican chocolate beater)

CINNAMON SHORTBREAD COOKIES
POLVORONES

250 g butter

½ cup (80 g) icing sugar

2¼ cups (280 g) plain flour, sifted

½ teaspoon ground cinnamon

¼ teaspoon salt

1 teaspoon vanilla essence

1 cup icing sugar mixed with 2 teaspoons
ground cinnamon

1 Beat butter until light and fluffy. Gradually add sugar, beating well after each addition, until creamy. Add flour, cinnamon, salt and vanilla and mix to form a stiff dough. Wrap in plastic wrap and chill for 2 hours.

2 Roll into small balls and flatten slightly or alternatively roll out dough on a lightly floured surface to 2 cm in thickness and cut out 5 cm rounds using a pastry cutter. Place on a greased oven tray and bake at 200°C (400°F) for 15 minutes or until lightly browned.

3 Roll warm cookies in sugar cinnamon mixture. Cool on wire rack and then dust again with remaining sugar mixture.

MAKES 25

CLAY POT COFFEE
CAFÉ DE OLLA

6 cups (1½ litres) water

½ cup (90 g) brown sugar

2 cinnamon sticks

4 whole cloves

½ cup (45 g) ground dark-roasted
ground coffee

1 Combine water, sugar, cinnamon and cloves in a saucepan. Bring to the boil, reduce heat and simmer gently for 15 minutes.

2 Stir in coffee and return to the boil for 1 minute longer. Strain and serve.

SERVES 4 TO 6

MEXICAN DOUGHNUTS
CHURROS

1 cup (125 g) plain flour, sifted

1 teaspoon salt

1 cup (250 ml) boiling water

1 egg

vegetable oil for cooking

1 slice white bread

½ lemon

icing sugar

1 Sift flour and salt into a mixing bowl. Make a well in the centre, add boiling water and whisk to a smooth batter. Add egg and beat until batter is smooth and shiny.

2 Heat oil in a large saucepan. When hot add bread and lemon and cook until bread is dark brown. Remove bread and lemon.

3 Spoon batter into a large piping bag fitted with a large star nozzle and pipe small logs, about 16 cm in length, directly into the hot oil. Cook until golden brown. Drain. Roll in icing sugar and serve warm.

MAKES 12

Cinnamon Shortbread Cookies

COFFEE WITH BRANDY AND ORANGE
CAFÉ DIABLO

1 wide strip orange rind

hot strong black coffee

1½ tablespoons brandy

whipped cream

1 Place orange rind in a cup, pour over coffee and add brandy and sugar to taste.
2 Top with whipped cream and serve immediately.

SERVES 1

ORANGES IN SYRUP
NARANJA EN DULCE

10 oranges

pinch salt

12 cups (3 litres) fresh orange juice

4 cups (1 litre) water

4 cups (1 kg) sugar

1½ cinnamon stick

1 Peel rind from oranges using a vegetable peeler. Discard peel. Cut oranges into quarters. Squeeze most of the juice from the oranges by pressing the corner edges towards each other. Reserve juice.
2 Place orange quarters and salt in a large saucepan and cover with water. Bring to the boil and simmer for 25 minutes.
3 Drain and rinse oranges. Place in a ceramic bowl, cover with water and set aside to soak for 8 hours, changing the water several times until the water remains clear.
4 Place water and orange juice, to make 16 cups (4 litres) liquid, in a saucepan. Add sugar and cinnamon and cook over a medium heat, stirring constantly, until sugar dissolves. Simmer for 1 to 1½ hours or until mixture forms a thick syrup.
5 Add oranges and cook a further 15 to 25 minutes or until oranges are golden, have absorbed some, syrup, and mixture is thick.
6 Serve oranges in syrup garnished with orange leaves, if desired.

SERVES 4

FLAMBÉED MANGOES
MANGOS DIABLO

20 g butter

1 tablespoon sugar

rind 1 lime or orange, cut into thick strips

3 tablespoons Triple Sec or similar orange liqueur

3 teaspoons fresh lime or orange juice

3 mangoes, peeled and sliced

2 tablespoons tequila

1 Melt butter in a heavy-based frypan. Add sugar and stir until dissolved. Add lime rind and liqueur and heat for 30 seconds then ignite. When flame dies down remove rind and add juice. Cook until it begins to thicken.
2 Add mangoes, bring back to the boil, add tequila and flame again.
3 Serve with vanilla ice cream or whipped cream.

SERVE 6

PAPAYA SORBET
SORBETE DE PAPAYA

½ cup (125 ml) fresh orange juice

1 tablespoon Grand Marnier or similar orange liqueur

¾ cup (185 g) sugar

1 tablespoon fresh lemon or lime juice

2 teaspoons finely grated lime or lemon rind

2 ripe papaya or pawpaw, peeled, seeded and puréed

1 Place orange juice, Grand Marnier, sugar, lime juice and rind in a saucepan and cook over medium heat, stirring constantly, until sugar dissolves. Bring to the boil. Simmer for 3 minutes. Remove from heat and set aside to cool.
2 Stir papaya purée through cooled sugar syrup.
3 Transfer mixture to a suitable freezer proof container, cover and freeze until sorbet starts to set around the outside.
4 Remove and beat until smooth. Freeze until set.

SERVES 6

Papaya Sorbet

Invariably a Mexican feast will finish with a platter of succulent fresh fruit. In Mexico street vendors meander through the markets and central squares selling ornately cut pineapples, oranges, watermelons and rockmelons. They always have chilli powder, salt, lime juice and salsas on hand, as Mexicans love their fruit laced with chilli.

FRESH FRUIT PLATTER
PLATON DE FRUTA FRESCA

1 large orange, peeled and thinly sliced

½ rockmelon (cantaloupe), seeded, peeled and cut into wedges

12 strawberries

1 small pineapple, peeled and cut into thin slices.

½ small watermelon, cut into thin slices

½ cup (125 ml) fresh lime juice

½ cup (45 g) grated fresh coconut (optional)

salt (optional)

chilli powder (optional)

salsas of your choice (optional)

1 Arrange fruit on a serving platter. Sprinkle with lime juice and coconut. Chill well.

2 Serve with accompaniments of your choice.

SERVES 6 TO 8

TEQUILA SUNRISE
TIJUANA TEQUILA DEL SOL

2 teaspoons grenadine

2 tablespoons crushed ice

1½ tablespoons tequila

3 tablespoons orange juice

soda water

1 Pour grenadine over crushed ice in a tall chilled glass.

2 Combine tequila and orange juice, pour over grenadine and then top with soda water.

SERVE 1

PINA COLADA

⅓ cup (80 ml) coconut milk

⅓ cup (80 ml) pineapple juice

⅓ cup (80 ml) light white rum

2 tablespoons crushed ice

1 slice pineapple

1 Place all ingredients except pineapple in a blender and blend until frothy.

2 Pour into a chilled glass and garnish with pineapple.

SERVES 1

TOMATO SANGRITA
SANGRITA DE TOMATE

3 tablespoons tomato juice

½ to 1 teaspoon grenadine (optional)

½ cup (125 ml) lemon or lime juice

1 teaspoon orange juice

pinch salt

crushed ice

½ birdseye chilli, seeded and chopped, or dash Tabasco sauce

½ teaspoons finely chopped fresh coriander

2 tablespoons tequila

1 Combine all ingredients except tequila, and shake well.

2 Add tequila and serve.

SERVES 1

SANGRITA MARIA (BLOODY MARY): Substitute 1½ tablespoons vodka for tequila, and squeeze extra juice from a wedge of lime over the cocktail before dropping it into the glass.

RED SANGRIA
SANGRIA ROJA

4 oranges, sliced

2 lemons, sliced

2 peaches, stoned, peeled and chopped

1 apple, cored, peeled and chopped

1 pear, cored, peeled and chopped

½ cup (125 g) sugar

½ cup (125 ml) brandy

2½ cups (625 ml) red wine

ice cubes

champagne or soda water

1 Place fruit in a punch bowl or sangria pitcher and sprinkle with sugar and brandy. Allow to stand overnight.

2 TO SERVE: Add wine and ice cubes. Add as much champagne as you wish or just enough soda water to add zest to the sangria.

SERVES 12

STRAWBERRY ATOLE
ATOLE DE FRESA

½ cup (60 g) dried masa or instant masa

1 tablespoon ground cinnamon

2 cups (500 ml) water

¾ cup (180 g) sugar

3 cups (750 ml) milk

¼ teaspoon vanilla essence

375 ml strawberry purée, made from fresh strawberries

1 cup (250 ml) cream

red food colouring (optional)

3 egg yolks

1 Place masa, cinnamon and water in a saucepan and cook over a medium heat, stirring constantly, until thickened.

2 Combine sugar and milk and stir until sugar dissolves. Add to masa mixture with vanilla, strawberry purée, cream and a few drops of food colouring. Mix well. Return to heat and simmer for 2 to 3 minutes, stirring constantly, or until thick.

3 Remove from heat. Add egg yolks one at a time, beating well after each addition. Return to and bring almost to the boil. Serve immediately.

SERVES 8

VARIATIONS: Substitute ¾ cup ground blanched almonds for strawberries and food colouring. Substitute raspberries for strawberries. Substitute 100 g dark chocolate, melted for strawberries and food colouring.

EGGNOG
ROMPOPE

This chilled drink can be served as a liqueur or even poured over fruit and ice cream. It was created by priests in the state of Peublo. You will find it served throughout Mexico, even to children, who love Rompope frozen as ice-blocks.

4 cups (1 litre) milk

1¼ cups (310 g) sugar

1 vanilla bean

10 egg yolks, well beaten

1½ cups (375 ml) brandy or white rum

1 Combine milk, sugar and vanilla bean in a saucepan and cook over a medium heat, stirring constantly until sugar dissolves. Bring to the boil, reduce heat and simmer, covered, for 20 minutes. Cool to room temperature.

2 Remove vanilla bean and gradually whisk egg yolks into milk mixture. Add brandy. Decant into sterilized bottles and seal tightly.

3 Keep refrigerated for at least 48 hours before serving.

SERVES 12

≈ GRENADINE

Grenadine is a syrup, made from pomegranate juice used to sweeten cocktails and desserts.

Left to right: Tequila Sunrise, Tequila Bloody Mary, Fruit Punch, Red Sangria, Pina Colada

LIME SQUASH
AGUA DE LIMON

8 cups (2 litres) water

1 cup (250 g) sugar

10 limes

2 cups (500 ml) crushed ice

1 Place water and sugar in a large pitcher and stir until sugar dissolves.

2 Finely grate rind of limes and squeeze limes. Add rind and juice to syrup.

3 Add crushed ice and serve in tall glasses.

SERVES 12

FRUIT PUNCH
CHICHA DE FRUTAS

½ teaspoons finely chopped fresh mint

⅔ cup (160 g) sugar

1 cup (250 ml) water

2 cinnamon sticks

12 whole cloves

2 cups (500 ml) pineapple juice

2 cups (500 ml) fresh orange juice

½ cup (125 ml) fresh lemon juice

⅓ cup (90 ml) fresh lime juice

ice cubes or frozen shapes made from pineapple, orange, lemon and lime

1 Combine mint and half the sugar, mix well.

2 Place in a saucepan with remaining sugar, water, cinnamon sticks and cloves. Bring to the boil, reduce heat, and simmer gently for 30 minutes. Strain through muslin or cheese-cloth. Add juices and mix well.

3 Serve well chilled with frozen ices.

MAKES 6 CUPS (1½ LITRES)

CREDIT: PINK GLASS AND JUG – ALBI IMPORTS; GLASSES – MEXICAN IMPORTS; SASH – CRAZY HORSE

MARGARITA

1½ tablespoons fresh lime juice

coarse salt

1½ tablespoons tequila

1½ tablespoons curacao or Cointreau

½ cup (125 ml) crushed ice

1 Moisten rim of serving glass with lime juice and dip in salt.

2 Place tequila, curacao, remaining lime juice and ice in a blender and blend until slushy.

3 Serve in prepared glass.

SERVES 1

NOTE: To make a frothy margarita add a spoonful of egg white before blending.

FRUIT MARGARITAS: Add a combination of fresh fruit, (strawberries, pineapple, mango or bananas) and blend with tequila, curacao, lime juice and ice. When making fruit margaritas there is no need to rim the glass with lime and salt.

TEQUILA BLOODY MARY
TEQUILA MARIA

1½ tablespoons tequila

¾ cup (180 ml) tomato juice

dash Tabasco sauce

dash Worcestershire sauce

½ teaspoons fresh lemon juice

1 teaspoon finely chopped fresh parsley, coriander, oregano or basil, slice lemon

stick of celery

1 Combine tequila, tomato juice, Tabasco sauce, Worcestershire sauce and lemon juice. Season to taste with freshly ground black pepper and salt.

2 Pour into a tall glass. Sprinkle with herb of your choice and serve garnished with lemon slice and celery stick.

SERVES 1

≈ TEQUILA

Mexico and tequila are inseparable. The sharp tangy liquor is made from the maguey cactus plant. But be careful, it is very potent. So serve plenty of antojitos with tequila. The piquant Mexican appetisers go well with this famous Mexican drinks. The easiest way to serve straight tequila is in small glasses with slices of lemon and a mound of coarse salt. Dip the lemon in the salt, savour its bite, then sip the tequila. Otherwise try a Margarita, a Tequila Sunrise or a Vallarta Fizz – all designed to set the tastebuds tingling and the senses reeling.

MEASURING MADE EASY

HOW TO MEASURE LIQUIDS

METRIC	IMPERIAL	CUPS
30 ml	1 fluid ounce	1 tablespoon plus 2 teaspoons
60 ml	2 fluid ounces	¼ cup
90 ml	3 fluid ounces	
125 ml	4 fluid ounces	½ cup
150 ml	5 fluid ounces	
170 ml	5 ½ fluid ounces	
180 ml	6 fluid ounces	¾ cup
220 ml	7 fluid ounces	
250 ml	8 fluid ounces	1 cup
500 ml	16 fluid ounces	2 cups
600 ml	20 fluid ounces (1 pint)	2 ½ cups
1 litre	1 ¾ pints	

HOW TO MEASURE DRY INGREDIENTS

15 g	1/2 oz	
30 g	1 oz	
60 g	2 oz	
90 g	3 oz	
125 g	4 oz	(¼ lb)
155 g	5 oz	
185 g	6 oz	
220 g	7 oz	
250 g	8 oz	(½ lb)
280 g	9 oz	
315 g	10 oz	
345 g	11 oz	
375 g	12 oz	(¾ lb)
410 g	13 oz	
440 g	14 oz	
470 g	15 oz	
500 g	16 oz	(1 lb)
750 g	24 oz	(1 ½ lb)
1 kg	32 oz	(2 lb)

QUICK CONVERSIONS

5 mm	¼ inch	
1 cm	½ inch	
2 cm	¾ inch	
2.5 cm	1 inch	
5 cm	2 inches	
6 cm	2 ½ inches	
8 cm	3 inches	
10 cm	4 inches	
12 cm	5 inches	
15 cm	6 inches	
18 cm	7 inches	
20 cm	8 inches	
23 cm	9 inches	
25 cm	10 inches	
28 cm	11 inches	
30 cm	12 inches	(1 foot)
46 cm	18 inches	
50 cm	20 inches	
61 cm	24 inches	(2 feet)
77 cm	30 inches	

NOTE: We developed the recipes in this book in Australia where the tablespoon measure is 20 ml. In many other countries the tablespoon is 15 ml. For most recipes this difference will not be noticeable.

However, for recipes using baking powder, gelatine, bicarbonate of soda, small amounts of flour and cornflour, we suggest you add an extra teaspoon for each tablespoon specified

USING CUPS AND SPOONS
All cup and spoon measurments are level

METRIC CUP				METRIC SPOONS	
¼ cup	60 ml	2 fluid ounces		¼ teaspoon	1.25 ml
⅓ cup	80 ml	2 ½ fluid ounces		½ teaspoon	2.5 ml
½ cup	125 ml	4 fluid ounces		1 teaspoon	5 ml
1 cup	250 ml	8 fluid ounces		1 tablespoon	20 ml

OVEN TEMPERATURES

TEMPERATURES	CELSIUS (°C)	FAHRENHEIT (°F)	GAS MARK
Very slow	120	250	½
Slow	150	300	2
Moderately slow	160-180	325-350	3-4
Moderate	190-200	375-400	5-6
Moderately hot	220-230	425-450	7
Hot	250-260	475-500	8-9

INDEX

SUPPLIERS

As indicated throughout the text, ingredients for Mexican cooking are available in a number of different places: be inventive, and explore all types of food outlets. Also, contact local Mexican restaurants to find their sources of supply.

For the recipes illustrated we used the following supplier:

SEÑOR NILA MEXICAN FOODS
2/6 Grosvenor Place
Brookvale   NSW   2100
Telephone: (02) 938 2274